Minute Musings

Spontaneous Combustions of Thought

Volume One

Daily Inspirational Messages
with
Scriptural References to Jesus Christ

compiled by

Philip M. Hudson

Copyright 2015 by Philip M. Hudson.
The book author retains sole copyright to his contributions to this book.

Published 2015.
Printed in the United States of America.

All rights reserved.

No portion of this book may be reproduced, stored in a retrieval system, or transmitted in any form or by any means – electronic, mechanical, photocopy, recording, scanning, or other – except for brief quotations in critical reviews or articles, without the prior written permission of the author.

ISBN 978-1-937862-98-5

Library of Congress Control Number 2015909163

This book was published by BookCrafters
Parker, Colorado.
bookcrafters@comcast.net

This book may be ordered from
www.bookcrafters.net
and other online bookstores.

Minute Musings

Spontaneous Combustions of Thought

Volume One

Daily Inspirational Messages
with
Scriptural References to Jesus Christ

Preface

Introduction..1

366 Inspirational Messages with Scriptural References to Jesus Christ.................5

Appendix One: Chronological List (Volume One)......................................373

Appendix Two: Alphabetical List (Volume One).......................................387

Appendix Three: Comprehensive Alphabetical Master List......................399

Appendix Four: Numerical List by Body of Scripture..............................459

About the Author...463

Also by the Author...465

Preface

Part of my motivation for compiling these three volumes has been the desire to create an opportunity for family groups to be "on the same page" in relation to at least one aspect of their religious experience. If every participant spent less than a minute reading a particular day's inspirational message about the Savior, perhaps the seeds that were planted could be nurtured in their minds as the day played out. Maybe knowing that they were pondering the same thoughts about the Savior, at the same time, would help to draw them closer together as a family. Perhaps they could even establish an on-going dialogue, as they shared with each other their unique perspectives relating to the daily topic of discussion.

I could have done an Internet search and come up with a pretty good list of the different scriptural references to the Savior. But going through the scriptures on my own voyage of discovery has been a wonderful experience. I did it lightning-fast, to be sure, but I really enjoyed it, and as I traveled through history page by page, it all seemed to tie together in an interesting way that had eluded me in the past.

I was also amazed to discover anew the profound witness of the Savior that permeates the Standard Works. It seemed that in every chapter, there were references to Him that I had somehow previously overlooked. It may be obvious to you, but I had not heretofore recognized the overwhelming testament of Jesus Christ that is found throughout the scriptures.

We are quite familiar with some of His name-titles and descriptions, and they easily roll off our tongues. We use them in our thoughts, prayers, testimonies, lessons, and conversations. Others are less obvious, but as I pondered them, I gained a greater appreciation of what may have been going through the minds of the prophets who recorded them as they received impressions and revelations. I began to understand that they had employed particular terminology in order to convey powerfully relevant messages. In just a few words, there were sermons to be studied. I realized that as we usually describe the Savior, we scarcely plumb the depths of His personality, and our gratitude for His mission only penetrates the surface layers of His divinity. I learned that I am only beginning to feel the impact His life has had on me, and to acknowledge its subtle influence on every aspect of my existence.

Finally, I thought of the observation of Nephi, who wrote: "We talk of Christ, we rejoice in Christ, we preach of Christ, we prophesy of Christ, and we write according to our prophecies, that our children may know to what source they may look for a remission of their sins." (2 Nephi 25:26). In the First Book of Nephi alone, he referred to the Savior in many ways, including The Lord God Almighty, The Messiah, The Lord our God, The God of Israel, The Savior of the World, The Lamb of God, Our Redeemer, The Son of the Everlasting God, The Son of the Eternal Father, The Eternal God, The God of Israel, and The Holy One of Israel, to name just a few. Each of these descriptions suggests that Nephi had more than just a superficial relationship with Jesus Christ. It would be great if these volumes could help us to know the Savior as he did.

Introduction

"What Think Ye of Christ?"
(Matthew 22:42).

This book is about our Lord and Savior Jesus Christ, His doctrine, and our application of His teachings in the modern world. Within its pages you will find 366 references to Him that are found in the scriptures, one for every day of the year, including February 29. Each includes a few lines of related text, intended to prompt you to remember Him throughout the day. The thoughts are intentionally brief, designed to provide an incentive for you to maintain the habit of consistent reflection, and to give you plenty of wiggle-room to thoughtfully expand upon the topic of the day, as you are moved upon by the Spirit to do so.

As I read the scriptures in my preparation to write the book, I was introduced to hundreds of intriguing nuances of expression by the prophets who testified of the Savior. Many familiar name-titles immediately caught my attention, as they undoubtedly have yours. I quickly realized that in these cases, holy men of God had received inspiration to use specific words that dramatically captured the essence of divine character traits that were germane to their related messages. These, I realized, must be revelatory name-titles that were intentionally and inseparably intertwined with prophetic insight and instruction, and I was amazed at how complimentary and mutually supportive the two seemed to be. I also found that the prophets tended to repeat themselves and each other, regularly borrowing favorite name-tiles from their contemporaries and from earlier writings, either quoting them verbatim or enhancing them slightly when they wanted to emphasize the threads of commonality that were woven into the foundation principles and doctrines that accompanied inspired instruction.

In fact, I discovered that there existed an amazing consistency and harmony betweeen the expressions of the prophets in the four Standard Works (the Bible, the Book of Mormon, the Doctrine and Covenants, and the Pearl of Great Price). As one would expect, all of those who contributed their own personal testament of Christ to these texts had a solid grasp of the divine nature of the Savior's mission, and manipulated language as an art form in order to be clear and persuasive, to relate more personally to their callings, to be true to their times, to touch the mystic chords of brotherhood that exist between all people, and to effectively address the spiritual needs of those whom they served.

In many cases, the Savor was portrayed in moving terms that contributed significantly to doctrinal and historical relevancy; however, the inclusion of these word-pictures in the scriptures seemed to be palpably less critical to the overall impact of the messages of the prophets and their reception by the people. These I would characterize as descriptions, rather than as name-titles. My testimony of the divine authenticity of the scriptures was strengthened with my realization that both name-titles and descriptions of the Savior reveal His nature in a new and refreshing light as they introduce multiple layers of His personality to our understanding, and as they clarify the applicability of holy writ to our circumstances. Name-titles and descriptions are sprinkled throughout the pages of this book like powdered sugar over a mouth-watering dessert, in no particular order or structure, although I have tried to make each one apropos to the topic at hand. The purpose of their inclusion is to invite the Spirit, add sweet savor, and enhance your benfit from, and enjoyment of, Minute Musings. As Peter Pan told Wendy: "All you need is faith, trust, and a little bit of pixie dust, and you can fly!"

The book does not pretend to comprise an exhaustive list. As a matter of fact, I initially envisioned creating just one volume, but as I became more heavily involved in my investigation of the scriptures, it soon became apparent that I would need to expand the scope of my efforts to at least three volumes. The appendices that follow the body of the text are designed to help you to quickly and easily navigate your way to your favorite name-titles and descriptions. They also extend an invitation to discover on your own many references to the Savior with which you may not have been familiar. Following Appendix Three are several pages that summon you to literally fill in the blanks with additional citations describing the nature and character of Jesus Christ. Doing so should personalize the book for you, strengthen your faith, reinforce your testimony of the Savior, and contribute to your more profound appreciation and application of the scriptures. Perhaps, at some point, there will be a need for a fourth, and even a fifth, volume that could represent our collaborative efforts.

Coming up with the list was actually the easy part. Writing the commentary was more challenging. I am sure I mis-stated myself more than once, or only awkwardly described a concept here or there. When you find a glaring example of my weakness in writing, remember that my age entitles me to a free pass every now and then. Give me the benefit of the doubt, and allow me to have a senior moment. Use my feeble effort as a springboard to launch your own more articulate interpretation of the signification of the particular name-title or description under consideration.

As you flip through Minute Musings, the physical symmetry of the layout of each page should be immediately apparent. When I put pen to paper, so to speak, I was struck by the need to bring balance and equilibrium to the thoughts that had crystalized in my mind. Striving to create artistry and proportion in phraseology was challenging, but it helped me to achieve a sense of stability that was at the same time refreshing and even stimulating. I believe that when we think of the Savior, and particularly when we record our impressions of Him, either for ourselves or for the benefit of others, He deserves our very best efforts, and for me, that meant creating something of not only intellectual and spiritual value, but also of aesthetic appeal.

I do know this. The Savior is the rudder of my ship, guiding me past unseen rocks and reefs. He is my helm, holding steady when winds of adversity blow. He is my telltale, alerting me to impending storms. He is my keel, helping me to move against the current and the wind. He is my mainsheet, holding firmly with just enough pressure to prevent me from capsizing when I am heeled over. He is my safety-line, providing security when my footing is unsure and the foaming sea is streaming across my deck. He is my compass, showing me the way, especially when the course is unclear. He is my chart, warning me of hidden dangers. He is my barometer, alerting me to impending storms. He is my sextant, orienting me not only to the stars, but also to eternity. He is my lookout, standing as my sentinel when I am distracted by trivial concerns. He holds the line that trails in my wake, offering safety when I fall overboard. He is the wind that fills my sails.

I testify of His ante-mortal existence, and of His foreordination to be the Redeemer of the world. The scriptures speak of His relationship with the Father, and of His divine investiture of authority. His appearances to His servants throughout history were many. The Book of Mormon, particularly, explains His condescension in taking a mortal body. Thus, I can better understand His temptations, and the power, might, dominion, and authority that typified His experience on the earth.

In His baptism, He demonstrated by example the way for me to follow. In His ministry, He taught the truths of the Gospel in simplicity. In the Garden of Gethsemane, He demonstrated His fortitude and compassion. The crucifixion, then, was only an apostrophe; His death but a pause to allow us to re-focus our attention on His resurrection and ascension into heaven.

He is my Advocate with the Father, and the Bread of Life. He is the Cornerstone of my creation, the Foundation of my existence. He is the Creator of worlds without number, and the Deliverer of the Covenant to all the children of our Father.

He is Emmanuel: truly, in Him God is with me. The Firstborn of the Spirit Children of the Father, He is Perfect in every detail. He is the Good Shepherd, and the Judge of both the quick and the dead. As Lord, King, and Jehovah, He has all power to act as our Mediator and as the Messenger of the Covenant.

The Lamb of God, He is the Messiah, the Anointed One, and my Redeemer. He is my Rock, and my Savior, the Only Begotten Son of God in the flesh. He is the Son of Man of Holiness, and my Second Comforter.

When He returns, it will be in the clouds. He will be accompanied by the Church of the Firstborn, and His Second Coming will usher in His Millennial Reign. For a thousand years, His Gospel will penetrate every soul and burn brightly in every bosom. I hope we will all be there to savor the experience together.

January 1

Wonderful
(Isaiah 9:6)

How shall He
be called, or how
can I describe Him?
My efforts exhaust
the reservoir of my
capacity to do so.
He is, in a word,
Wonderful.

January 2

The Judge of all the Earth
(Genesis 18:25)

In the midst of
confusion and turmoil,
and corruption in high places,
there is One who rules above all
others, who is eminently fair,
and undeviatingly true,
even **The Judge of
all the Earth**.

January 3

A Righteous Man
(Luke 23:47)

His life is our pattern and His teachings are the expression of His holy calling. The names by which He is described are numerous. But above all the rest, stands this simple certainty: He is **A Righteous Man**.

January 4

The
Fear of God
(Genesis 20:11)

We acknowledge
His inspired leadership,
recognize His authority, and
emulate His example. We meekly
accept both the rewards for obedience
as well as the consequences for willful
neglect of our responsibilities. He
is **The Fear of God**.

January 5

He that hath the Key of David
(Revelation 3:7)

The Saints reflect the everlasting light, and are as beacons to those seeking the truth. Even as saviors on Mount Zion, both to the living and to the dead, they are missionary companions to **He that hath the Key of David**.

January 6

The Everlasting God
(Isaiah 40:28)

I am drawn
to the Mountain of
the Lord's House, to fire
and smoke in the home of **The
Everlasting God**, the Great I Am.
There I will be endowed at the hands
of the priesthood. Those with its
authority shall anoint my head
with oil and I will consecrate
to the Father my efforts to
assist in establishing
Zion.

January 7

The Mighty One of Jacob
(Isaiah 60:16)

"It is excellent to have a giant's strength, but it is tyrannous to use it like a giant." (Shakespeare, "Measure for Measure"). Christ, **The Mighty One of Jacob** knows that power and violence are mutually exclusive, and that when one is present, the other is absent.

January 8

(He) Who Gave Himself for our Sins
(Galatians 1:4)

"Who is that Samaritan?" The question is asked in a contemptuous tone of voice. "What reasons would compel his ministrations? He performs his works only to be seen of men!" While quietly watching from a distance, He **Who Gave Himself for our Sins** weeps at his selfless charitable acts.

January 9

The Word of Life
(1 John 1:1)

We
were
born to die
at the conclusion
of our mortal experience.
However, the promise of **The Word of Life** is that death does not extinguish the light. Rather, it puts out one lamp as we welcome a brighter day.

January 10

The Lord
He is God
(Deuteronomy 4:35)

Just as the piercing sound of the ram's horn sent an unmistakable message to an unbelieving and skeptical Jericho, so too do we testify before the world without equivocation: **The Lord He is God**.

January 11

He (Who) is Able to Save ...to the Uttermost
(Hebrews 7:25)

Wounds heal
when cared for properly.
Because Jesus Christ is **Able
to Save to the Uttermost**, we can
learn from our mistakes and
gain valuable experience,
even as we rely upon
Him to redeem us
from our
sins.

January 12

The Lord from Heaven
(1 Corinthians 15:47)

The Lord from Heaven
came down to earth, to live
among men and suffer temptation.
We, too, left that same holy habitation,
to gain experience, develop faith,
and walk in obedience to the
commandments.

January 13

The Prophet
of Nazareth
(Matthew 21:11)

Humility
is that magnificent
celestial quality possessed
by **The Prophet of Nazareth**,
Who was endowed with great
power through intimate familiarity
with the Spirit. We can also draw upon
that same Source from which all truth
flows if we come to the altar of faith
and prostrate ourselves before
Him bearing the sacrifice of
a broken heart and a
contrite spirit.

January 14

He Who was Prepared from the Foundation of the World
(Ether 3:14)

Silver and gold are representative of idolatry. When the Savior is sold for such, the symbolism is clear. We betray Christ when the things of the world become our obsession and we ignore Him **Who was Prepared from the Foundation of the World**.

January 15

Counsellor
(Isaiah 9:6)

To whom
may I bare my soul
and with confidence share
my feelings? To my **Counsellor**
and to my Comforter, Who knows
my thoughts and penetrates my
heart. He will gently respond
to my inner groanings, and
will apply the soothing
Balm of Gilead to
my wounds.

January 16

Rabbi
(John 1:38)

Rabbi,
Who knowest
all things, do not
send a famine into
the land, but grant that
we may live in Bethlehem.
For Thy holy habitation
is as a house of bread,
where we may freely
partake of Thy
word.

January 17

The Carpenter
(Mark 6:3)

The Carpenter was familiar with wood. He understood its blemishes and its imperfections, and knew that the intense heat from a kiln would improve the quality of the materials with which He worked. He gauged the strengths and weaknesses of each piece, and saw that if they would bond together they would be stronger than when they stood alone. He also had the capacity to envision the finished products, and knew that they would bear little resemblance to the raw materials from which they had been made.

January 18

The
Bread of Life
(John 6:35)

The Stick of Judah
nourishes the Gentiles,
as manna in the wilderness
of their journey to Christ, while
the Stick of Joseph strengthens
the Lamanites, as **The Bread
of Life** to a branch that
has grown up and
over the wall.

January 19

The
Great King
(Malachi 1:14)

Nature is all about balance, for there must be opposites in both the physical and the spiritual worlds. Some are good, some are neutral, and some are bad. There are men and women, and right and wrong. There are life and death, good and evil, holiness and wickedness, sense and insensibility, pleasure and pain, and happiness and misery. There is **The Great King** Who rules in the heavens, and the devil whose dominion is hell.

January 20

The Lord the Righteous Judge
(2 Timothy 4:8)

At the Bar of Justice, **The Lord the Righteous Judge** will not only evaluate the sum total of our acts, and look at what we have done while on the earth. He will also more seriously consider the effect of those acts, and examine what we have become.

January 21

The
Word
(John 1:1)

The Word is written
in our hearts, and our native
tongue is the language of the spirit.
His commandments are woven into our
sinews, and stitched into the very
fabric of the tapestry
of our lives.

January 22

The Lord our God
is One Lord
(Deuteronomy 6:4)

Amid myriad
evidences of God,
in the vistas of nature
and the pulsing rhythms
of the ebb and flow of
life, know this and
be not deceived:
**The Lord our
God is One
Lord**.

January 23

The
Brazen Serpent
(Helaman 8:14)

The Brazen Serpent looms before us, as we eat, drink, and make merry in a union with spiritual Babylon. It is so easy to look beyond the Mark that is provided as our standard.

January 24

The Strength of
the Children of Israel
(Joel 3:16)

Those who plan
for adversity are blessed,
for they know this: **The Strength
of the Children of Israel** will surely
smite the earth with strife and famine.
Only those Saints who walk in His
way will prosper. In spite of their
hardships, they will rejoice in
the blessings that follow
obedience.

January 25

(Him Who)
Suffered without the Gate
(Hebrews 13:12)

The vision
of the Tree of Life
can be a focus of our faith,
leading us to an appreciation
of Him Who **Suffered without
the Gate**. It can prepare us for our
own personal struggles with the
swirling mists of opposition
shrouding the path where
so many others have
lost their way.

January 26

The Father
of Lights
(James 1:17)

In the
midst of the
trials in our lives,
we beg for forgiveness.
Our experience has a dark
side, as evil influences jockey for
position to command our undivided
attention. The Gospel Plan, however,
is merciful, granting us favor with
The Father of Lights, even as we
struggle onward through the
dancing shadows toward
the brighter day.

January 27

Amen
(John 14:6)

As
I thank
Him for His
gracious blessings,
I murmur **Amen** and
Amen. When I utter His
Holy Name, and reverently
marvel at His majesty, I
wonder how I can ever
truly express my
gratitude.

January 28

Excellent
is Thy Name
(Psalms 8:1)

Lord,
strengthen us.
The tares are so fresh,
so succulent, and so inviting.
But it is a poisonous gift that awaits
the unwary, for the mature plant is
deceiving. How much better it is
to be nourished by Living
Bread, for **Excellent is**
His **Name**.

January 29

The Prince of Life
(Acts 3:15)

The Prince of Life works by addition, rather than by subtraction, and promises us the bestowal of many sheaves. As we learn to subdue our carnal nature by nurturing the spark of divinity within ourselves, He progressively endows us with greater spiritual powers until we finally bask in an eternal light.

January 30

A
Nazarene
(Matthew 2:23)

He was from
a little town that was
way off the beaten track. The
one that's made fun of, where people
used to live before they pulled up stakes
and moved to the big city. He was from a
place were young men go into the trades instead
of going on to college to receive higher education
and the opportunity to consider lucrative career
options. He came from the working class
where not much changes and there are
few surprises; where folks work
hard just to get by with the
necessities of life. He
was **A Nazarene**.

January 31

The First and the Last
(Isaiah 44:6)

Whisperings
that are inarticulate
and yet are strangely familiar
enlarge my soul with understanding
as the Still Small Voice washes over me
to soothe and comfort me with feelings of
peace. My vision expands as flashes of
insight burst forth from the deepest
recesses of memory. Beyond my
limited horizons, I sense the
presence of Him Who is
ever before my face,
**The First and
the Last**.

February 1

A Star
out of Jacob
(Numbers 24:17)

His ways are strait
and His course is fixed.
The trajectory of His path
soars over all His creations.
And to the faithful, He is, as
it were, **A Star out of Jacob**
to guide them unerringly
beyond every diversion
toward a safe haven.

February 2

The God of
my Salvation
(Psalms 18:46)

He is my
deliverance, and
He will never fail me
nor deny me a place at His
table. I have His assurance
that He is, and forever
will be, **The God of
my Salvation**.

February 3

The Sun of Righteousness
(Malachi 4:2)

We keep our faces
oriented toward the light
and feel the enveloping love
of **The Sun of Righteousness**.
As we bask in its warmth, our
resolve to remain His faithful
servants is revitalized.

February 4

The Creator of
the Ends of the Earth
(Isaiah 40:28)

We stand in awe of
our surroundings, and as we
try to make sense of the mystery, a
Still Small Voice whispers quietly to us,
assuring us of our heavenly lineage.
Though seemingly unfathomable,
we ponder the works of God,
**The Creator of the Ends
of the Earth**.

February 5

The Brightness of God's Glory
(Hebrews 1:3)

He is a beacon, the bonfire of our inspiration, Whose radiance draws us to Him. **The Brightness of God's Glory** is our guiding light that will lead us all the way to our heavenly home.

February 6

Lord God of
the Holy Prophets
(Revelation 22:6)

Give us the
strength to endure to
the end, and the power
to resist Satan's enticements.
Oh, our **Lord God of the Holy
Prophets**, let us turn to their
inspired counsel and heed
their warning voices
before it is too late
and the day of
redemption
is past.

February 7

The Lord is our Judge;
the Lord is our Lawgiver
(Isaiah 33:22)

The Lord is our Judge; the Lord is our Lawgiver, and so the Light of Christ has been given to every babe who comes innocently into the world, so that all might be provided with one undisputable, irreproachable, and inimitable standard against which correct choices might be made in an atmosphere of free will.

February 8

The Root and
the Offspring of David
(Revelation 22:16)

He is both **The Root and the Offspring of David**, and is of royal lineage equally in heaven and on earth, by heritage both the King of the Jews and a peer of the realm of celestial glory.

February 9

Holy, Holy, Holy
(Isaiah 6:3)

What superlatives can match our emotion as we express our adoration of God? Language seems so inadequate and feelings defy description. Isaiah may have put it best. He is **"Holy, Holy, Holy."**

February 10

Jesus Christ of Nazareth
(Acts 4:10)

He was not just the son of a carpenter, and not only the sagacious teacher some have supposed Him to be. He was the Anointed One, **Jesus Christ of Nazareth**.

February 11

(Him Who) is Passed into the Heavens
(Hebrews 4:14)

Many commemorate the death of Christ. There are only a few who celebrate His life. Fewer still are willing to pattern their lives after Him Who **is Passed into the Heavens**.

February 12

(Him Who) Healed the People
(2 Chronicles 30:20)

We
lose our focus
on the Brazen Serpent,
as we eat, drink, and make
merry in a union with Spiritual
Babylon. We look beyond the
Mark, never raising our
eyes to Him Who
**Healed the
People**.

February 13

A Minister of the Circumcision for the Truth of God
(Romans 15:8)

What are we to do? How can we find the truth? To whom may we turn for guidance and direction? Are the heavens silent? Does God no longer speak to us? We testify that the Lord is near, and is ever **A Minister of the Circumcision for the Truth of God**.

February 14

Abba, Father
(Mark 14:36)

In the midst of
our extremity, we cry
out, **Abba**, **Father**, to Him
Who is the one source of
comfort when we have
exhausted all other
avenues, and they
have proven
hopeless.

February 15

God, the Greatest of All
(Doctrine & Covenants 19:18)

President,
Prime Minister,
Pope, and Priest are titles
that would seem to convey a
sense of authority. What of Him
Who abased Himself and washed
the feet of the Apostles? Is not
He our **God the Greatest
of All**?

February 16

The Lord
that Healeth
Exodus 15:26

The world is
slowly dying of spiritual thirst
in the deserts of Babylon. The guilty
grovel in swirling clouds of dust that have
been stirred up by their own indiscretions, their
throats parched by the unremitting onslaught of a
sweltering sandstorm of sin. They are unaware that
redemption and restoration are just a single hydro-
therapy session away. The experience cannot be
purchased with money. It simply awaits our
discovery in cool, cleansing, and curative
waters. The ordinance of baptism quietly
acknowledges our faith in **The Lord
that Healeth** our infirmities.

February 17

A
Living Stone
(1 Peter 2:4)

The
Lord Jesus is
A Living Stone, a
Rock and a Foundation
on Whom we may lean to
rest our weary bones. He is
the One from Whom we may
draw strength. He is our
Sure Support and our
Anchor to the
Infinite.

February 18

A
Righteous Judge
(2 Timothy 4:8)

At
the Bar
of God, when
life is measured
and all eternity hangs
in the balance, it will be
comforting to realize
that He who holds
our destiny in His
own hands is **A
Righteous
Judge**.

February 19

The
First Begotten
(Hebrews 1:6)

**The
First Begotten**
Son of God was the greatest of our Father's children, foreordained from before the foundation of the world to ransom us through the Atonement from the seemingly unalterable demands of Justice.

February 20

(Him Who) Taste(d) Death for every Man
(Hebrews 2:9)

While we
can be certain that
everyone must die, it
is equally clear that few
really take the time to live.
Only when we are alive to
our eternal possibilities
do we appreciate Him
Who **Tasted Death
for every
Man**.

February 21

(Him who is) Counted Worthy of More Glory Than Moses
(Hebrews 3:3)

The great
lawgiver spoke
to Jehovah on Sinai
and received the tablets
of stone. His face shone as
the sun at noonday, but He
obediently loosed the latchets
of his shoes in the stunning
presence of Him Who is
**Counted Worthy of
More Glory than
Moses**.

February 22

The
Hope of Israel
(Acts 28:20)

We
anticipated
before our birth that
the Plan would provide that
the yoke of the faithful would be easy,
and the burdens they would carry would
be light. Repentance would take away
the sting, and **The Hope of Israel**
would leave sweet savor
in its place.

February 23

The Beginning and the End
(Revelation 22:13)

My
joy is full,
and with gladness
I lift up mine eyes unto
the Lord. Because the horizon
of my sight is eternal, I look with
joy, anticipation, and expanded
vision to Him Who is both
**The Beginning and
the End**.

February 24

The Lord God
of Hosts
(Isaiah 10:24)

With
their banners
unfurled and trumpets
resounding, the armies of
Israel meet the foe on the field
of battle. **The Lord God of Hosts**
Who leads His people, bears
both the signs and tokens
of His fearsome
power.

February 25

The Head of Every Man
(1 Corinthians 11:3)

"O God, that men should put an enemy in their mouths to steal away their brains!" (Shakespeare, "Othello"). How much better it is to be in command of our thoughts, words, and deeds; to yield our minds, and our hearts, and our strength to **The Head of Every Man**.

February 26

(He Who Upholds) all Things by the Word of His Power
(Hebrews 1:3)

When we reach the critical juncture of dedication, discipline, and devotion, a perfect storm of the spirit is created. He Who Upholds **all Things by the Word of His Power** is able to make intercession for each of the sons and daughters of God.

February 27

An Example
(John 13:15)

When
the Savior's love
is reflected in our actions,
and others see our works, their
thoughts should turn to Him, for to
Him belongs the credit. His life is our
greatest **Example**. Even His most
pious disciples are not worthy
to unloose the latchets
of His shoes.

February 28

The God
of Beth-el
(Genesis 31:13)

Sinai is
not a place, but is
an attitude. The faithful see
fire in every common bush, and
universally acknowledge the divine
presence of **The God of Beth-el** in His
earthly sanctuaries. They recognize
that all the world is His holy
habitation, and therefore
they tread carefully on
its sacred ground.

February 29

The King, Whose Name is the Lord of Hosts
(Jeremiah 46:18)

The King, Whose Name is the Lord of Hosts, has paid the tuition for our enrollment in the school of hard knocks. Its curriculum will reinforce what we learned in spiritual kindergarten. Any detours and disappointments that we experience along the way are in reality just bumps and potholes beside the strait and narrow path. As long as we remain enrolled in God's Driver Education Program, He will recognize our learner's permit that allows us to grind the gears and even run a few red lights as we lurch along on the road that leads back home.

March 1

He (Who) is Able to Succor Them that are Tempted
(Hebrews 2:18)

Jesus was physically lifted up upon the cross, was figuratively lifted up as a light to the world, and spiritually lifted up to heaven as a glorified being. He has tremendous power to draw us unto Him, and exerts an authoritative influence over our lives. Thus, **He is Able to Succor them that are Tempted**.

March 2

The Beloved
Son of God
(Matthew 3:17)

As He came up out of
the waters of baptism at Jordan,
His Father smiled across the expanse
of eternity, and announced His pleasure
at the token of obedience. After all,
Jesus was **The Beloved
Son of God**.

March 3

(Him Who) Learned Obedience by the Things which He Suffered
(Hebrews 5:8)

We endure
to the end in order to
develop confidence and to
grow in faith and knowledge.
As we face trials and tribulations,
we keep in fond remembrance, and
follow the example of, the Savior
of the World, Who **Learned
Obedience by the Things
Which He Suffered**.

March 4

The
Lord Jesus
(Luke 24:3)

Gratitude is
more than appreciation
and is greater than thanks. It
is independent of circumstances,
is founded on faith, and shapes
our engagement with God.
It is a celestial quality
that binds us to
**The Lord
Jesus**.

March 5

(He) Who
Gave Himself For Us
(Titus 2:14)

He Who Gave Himself For Us knows that "every man goes down to his death bearing in his hands only that which he has given away." (Persian Proverb).

March 6

The Only Begotten Son
(John 1:14)

We are
all born of flesh
and blood, and our fathers
and mothers are rooted within
the family of man. There is, however,
another, born of a mortal mother,
Who is the Holiest of All, even
The Only Begotten Son of
the immortal Father
of Spirits.

March 7

The
King Eternal
(1 Timothy 1:17)

Marriage
between a man
and a woman is the
basic building block of
eternity. It represents the
highest expression of not only
our individual lives, but also our
interdependency. It is ordained of
God, and is the sure foundation
of every family that has been
created by the power
and the authority
of **The King
Eternal**.

March 8

(He Who is) Without Sin unto Salvation
(Hebrews 9:28)

Only God
is in a position
to look out across
the wide expanse of
all eternity, upon all of
His mighty creations, and
pronounce them "good."
For only He is **Without
Sin unto Salvation**.

March 9

The Only Wise God our Savior
(Jude 1:25)

Vibrant testimonies are borne amid myriad evidences of His love. He is revealed through the Holy Ghost as **The Only Wise God our Savior**.

March 10

The
Consolation of Israel
(Luke 2:25)

Jesus Christ is
The Consolation of Israel.
Long ago, Isaiah counseled His
chosen people to forsake the apostasy
that had for so long been their recurring
inclination. For they had been brought
home to the safety and security of
a covenant relationship with
their Master.

March 11

God the Judge of All
(Hebrews 12:23)

Our nature in our fallen state is to be subject to the influences of Satan. When we have no direct or indirect experience with the Divine, when we are alienated from God by spiritual death, we become carnal, sensual, and devilish. This is why, from the Fall of Adam, **God the Judge of All** has provided us with the Plan of Salvation, that mortality might be a preparatory state that allows us to develop the qualities required for a reconciliation with our Father in Heaven.

March 12

The
Son of David
(Matthew 12:23)

**The
Son of David**
never strayed far
from His homeland
that would one day be
called Holy. How fitting
that it would be from a little
town of no consequence, from
Bethlehem, the House of Bread,
that all who hungered would
find spiritual nourishment.

March 13

The
Light of Men
(John 1:4)

We
grope about
in the shadows that
are a part of life, and struggle
to light a match of our own making.
We think that we can somehow illuminate
the way before us and change the long night
of darkness into day. While just beyond the
horizon of our sight, **The Light of Men**
waits for an invitation to cheer our
lives with His influence, so that
we may confidently walk
in the brightness of
His glory.

March 14

The True Light, which Lighteth every Man
(John 1:9)

Our agitated search for happiness is very much like a butterfly. The more we chase after it, the more it seems to elude us. But if we forget ourselves, and turn our attention to selfless acts of service and quiet Christianity, happiness will come and rest gently on our shoulder. Our example is **The True Light, which Lighteth every Man**.

March 15

Living Water
(John 4:10)

I am thankful
for the opportunities
I am given to serve my
brothers and sisters and to
grow in His grace. I know that
I must draw upon **Living Water** if
I hope to refresh my wisdom, insight,
and understanding. As I drink deeply
at His oasis and quench my thirst, I
shall praise His name before the
congregation of the faithful
for His goodness
and mercy.

March 16

The
Lord of Glory
(James 2:1)

During His
ministry, each time
He prayed to His Father,
He provided the perfect pattern
for us to follow. He, Who is **The
Lord of Glory**, left a message
that is unmistakable: Let
him who would be
master, be the
servant of
all.

March 17

The Surety of
a Better Testament
(Hebrews 7:22)

Our
developing faith
in Him Who is **The Surety
of a Better Testament** helps us
all to understand this simple guiding
principle: "The best and most beautiful
things in the world cannot be seen
or even touched. They must
be felt with the heart."
(Helen Keller).

March 18

(He Who) Came into the World to Save Sinners
(1 Timothy 1:15)

His legacy was not only that He was a great teacher. His fortune was not merely to be a philosopher. He lived righteously, avoiding every offense, and His days and years were perfect, as would be expected from one Who **Came into the World to Save Sinners** from spiritual death.

March 19

Christ,
the Chosen of God
(Luke 23:35)

As conflicting ideologies
grated against each other, and
as sparks began to fly, the drums
of war were heard in Heaven. In the
battle raging in the hearts of men, it
was **Christ, the Chosen of God**
Who stood with the valiant
sons and daughters of
His Father to face
the adversary.

March 20

The Bridegroom
(Matthew 9:15)

Forgive me for coming to the wedding feast without having first made the necessary preparations. As I now strugge in sackcloth and with ashes to regain the favor of **The Bridegroom**, I feel His tender mercies, even as I recognize my own inadequacies and resolve to reform my behavior.

March 21

Jesus
the Son of God
(Hebrews 4:14)

Is **Jesus the Son of God**? It is the one question that divides us into camps that are diametrically opposed. For there are, save, two churches only, and we need to choose one, or the other. We are either for Him, or we are against Him.

March 22

The Strength of Israel
(1 Samuel 15:29)

The wicked
shrink in fear before
the terrible banners of Zion,
retreating from the presence of the
Spirit, even as the Saints, who draw
upon **The Strength of Israel**, are
infused with His power.

March 23

The Savior
Jesus Christ
(Mormon 3:14)

Those
who have
no knowledge
of **The Savior Jesus
Christ** are held captive
and are blinded to the
ways of the Lord
that are before
their eyes.

March 24

The
God of Israel
(2 Nephi 25:14)

We have been promised a peace that surpasses understanding. Where can we find the key to that happiness? The simple truth is that in **The God of Israel** our needs are satisfied.

March 25

God's Anointed
(Acts 4:27)

At the
Great Council,
God's Anointed came
forward as a bright and shining
morning star, a beacon, even then, to
lead us unto Him. When conflicting
ideologies competed for attention,
He was there to sustain those
who stood and expressed
their desire to uphold
the Merciful Plan
of our Father.

March 26

The King
(Isaiah 6:5)

Mansions
have been prepared
for those who wait patiently on
The King of heaven. Each habitation
has been crafted to suit our circumstances
and meet our individual needs. Set
your sights high, then. Not
failure, but low aim
is crime.

March 27

The
Chosen of God
(John 23:35)

The Savior was
The Chosen of God,
the very prototype of the
perfection that is an attainable
goal for each of us. His Gospel is
the key that breaks down the barriers
to our personal progress. Without
the energizing influence of His
divine intervention and His
nurturing care, we are
doomed to failure.

March 28

The Father of Heaven and of Earth
(2 Nephi 25:12)

Unavoidably,
we all face a coming
separation of time and
space, and we fear the pain
it may bring. But there are other
qualities that strengthen our resolve.
These are the divine characteristics
of our Heavenly Father that dispel
our anxiety, dismiss our fears, and
create a tangible bridge reaching
all the way to eternity. We are
one with Him Who loves us:
**The Father of Heaven
and of Earth.**

March 29

A Merciful and Faithful High Priest
(Hebrews 2:17)

Knowledge
gained in this life
will rise with us in the
resurrection, bringing with it
an advantage in our life to come.
The future embraces the promise that
we may obtain perfect knowledge,
which is the understanding that
comes by exercising our own
saving faith in **A Merciful
and Faithful High
Priest**.

March 30

The
Great Jehovah
(Doctrine & Covenants 128:9)

The
purpose
of our existence
is to develop qualities
that are in perfect harmony
with the divine nature of
our Lord and Savior
who is Jesus Christ,
even **The Great
Jehovah**.

March 31

The
True Vine
(John 15:1)

Our
experiences
are sure to bring us
trials. However, if we
are deeply rooted in the
rich soil of the Gospel,
we will grow and
flourish with
**The True
Vine**.

April 1

(He Who) Sitteth on the Right Hand of God
(Colossians 3:1)

How can we be sure that our prayers are heard by our Father Who dwells in heaven? Our Intercessor there, in Whose name we may approach the celestial throne, is He Who **Sitteth on the Right Hand of God**.

April 2

The High and Lofty One
that Inhabits Eternity
(Isaiah 57:15)

The
mortal ministry of
**The High and Lofty One
that Inhabits Eternity** is proof
enough that we were created in the
image and likeness of God. Quiet
stirrings within us confirm that
we have not only the same
physical characteristics
as our Parents, but we
also have the same
spiritual traits.

April 3

(Him Who was) Raised from the Dead
(2 Timothy 2:8)

Within every heart
beats the same silent question:
Will we live beyond the grave? The
answer has been given with finality by
Him Who was **Raised from the Dead**
when He said that if we would look
to God, faith would replace fear,
and we would be alive in
Christ.

April 4

Creator of Israel
(Isaiah 43:15)

Creator of Israel,
forgive those who walk
in darkness, and who know
not where to find the truth. For
those who helplessly endure the
night suffer the pain and anguish
of spiritual blindness. With Thy
grace, however, they may
yet be healed, so that
they, too, may see
the light.

April 5

The Lord the
God of Heaven
(Jonah 1:9)

The Lord the God of Heaven was endowed by His Father with the priesthood keys of eternal life. Nevertheless, He clothed Himself in mortal clay and died on a cross so that, one day, we might live with Him in His Kingdom.

April 6

The Bright
and Morning Star
(Revelation 22:16)

The heavens
bear a powerful
witness of God's majesty.
For its most luminous object
is that **Bright and Morning Star**,
a beacon to the faithful as they chart
their course, giving His assurance
that He is a Celestial Body that
looms large just beyond the
horizon of their sight, but
within the easy grasp
of their vision.

April 7

Jehovah, the Eternal Judge
(Moroni 10:34)

When **Jehovah, the Eternal Judge** comes in the clouds with His Saints, it will be at one and the same time great and dreadful. For the righteous, it is the day when Christ will reveal His marvelous power. For the unrighteous, however, it will be a terrible day of reckoning, for they will feel the wrath of His indignation.

April 8

The
Son of God
(Romans 1:4)

With a
crown of platted
thorns that comprised
a cruel counterpoint, the
words were spat out: He is
the King of the Jews. Now
with the greatest reverence
and incomprehensible
significance is the title
of honor uttered by
the faithful, who
recognize Him
as **The Son
of God**.

April 9

(He Who) Died and Rose Again
(1 Thessalonians 4:14)

He Who Died and Rose Again set the example for each of us to follow. "Cowards, die many times before their deaths. The valiant never taste of death but once." (Shakespeare, "Julius Caesar").

April 10

Jesus Christ
the Righteous
(1 John 2:1)

**Jesus Christ
the Righteous** is He Who
trod the winepress alone. He did
not shirk the agony of Gethsemane, the
humiliation that followed in the court of Pilate,
or the pain He endured on the lonely hill of Calvary.
All along the way, during His greatest trials, He
was attended by angels who were drawn
to His virtue and who faithfully
ministered to His
needs.

April 11

The Savior
of the World
(John 4:42)

In dazzling white, we shall
present ourselves in the clouds before
Him Who appears dressed in robes of scarlet.
Cleansed of sin, we shall ascend into His Presence,
even as our thoughts turn to a lonely winepress
and blood sprinkled on spotless garments.
He is **The Savior of the World**, and
we are washed clean through
His sacrifice.

April 12

The Zeal of
the Lord of Hosts
(2 Kings 19:31)

Who is **The Zeal of the Lord of Hosts**? We ponder the question, and reflect upon the Master, Who draws close to His disciples and succors His people, sustaining even His children upon the isles of the sea. His name shall be called Wonderful, Counsellor, The Mighty God, The Everlasting Father, for He is our Strength, and our Protector, and our Guide, and our Friend.

April 13

The Word of God
(Revelation 19:13)

If we
desire to know
The Word of God, we
must embrace His true doctrine,
which is to believe in Him and repent.
Then we must be baptized for the remission
of our sins with the ordinance approved by
the Savior Himself, and performed by His
ordained servants whose priesthood
authority traces directly
back to Him.

April 14

The
Great God
(Titus 2:13)

We have been asked by
none other than **The Great God**
to press forward through the gloom
of temporal darkness, to be His disciples,
and to endure to the end, whenever that
might be, or wherever it might take
us, and at whatever the cost.

April 15

The
Anointed One
(Psalms 2:2)

From the Garden
our first parents tended,
to the fire and smoke high on
Sinai, down through the years to
a lonely hill and a borrowed tomb;
to our day, and to a millennial dawn,
He was, and is, and forever will
be, **The Anointed One**.

April 16

The Author and Finisher of our Faith
(Hebrews 12:2)

Our testimonies
are hewn from a quarry of
stone and are solid foundations
upon which we may build our belief.
Sustain us, uphold us, and defend us,
Thou **Author and Finisher of our Faith**!

April 17

The
Mighty God
(Isaiah 9:6)

As disciples
of **The Mighty God,**
we have crossed over Jordan.
We stand with Joshua, who said:
"Choose you this day whom ye will
serve, but as for me and my house,
we will serve the Lord."
(Joshua 24:15).

April 18

The
Image of God
(2 Corinthians 4:4)

In His
sermons, with
His parables, and by His
own example, the Lord gives
a revelation of His character; an
autobiographical thread that leads
back to His Father. We have been
given a blueprint to follow,
upon which is engraven
**The Image Of
God**.

April 19

Jesus of Galilee
(Matthew 26:69)

He chose a fisherman who was acqainted with tempests, was unafraid of wind or waves, and who trusted his instincts. He chose a fisherman, who was accustomed to casting his net, believing that his efforts would be fruitful. He chose a fisherman, because He was, after all, **Jesus of Galilee**.

April 20

The Judge of Quick and Dead
(Acts 10:42)

It is **The Judge of Quick and Dead** Who is our Redeemer. Those who reject His power unto salvation cannot hope to progress eternally, but instead will come to know with chilling clarity what it really means to be damned.

April 21

A Serpent
of Brass
(Alma 33:19)

His
life was
His message,
and He healed the
sick better than any
physician. He was as
A Serpent of Brass, a
caduceus, Who promised
that those who would look
to Him in faith might be
healed, and live.

April 22

He
is Good
(Psalms 34:8)

He is Good,
and He hates sin
because of what it does
to the transgressor. When
they are redeemed through
His Atonement, however,
and are saved by His
grace, the righteous
will shine as the
sun, in His
kingdom.

April 23

A
Righteous Branch
(Jeremiah 23:5)

I am
resolute in my
determination to
make daily scripture
study a priority. Though
many distractions compete
for my attention, if I but flex
my spiritual muscles to reach
out and grasp **A Righteous
Branch**, I know that He
will support me,
even in my
frailties.

April 24

Apostle
(Hebrews 3:1)

We must
heed the counsel to
lengthen our stride and
to redouble our efforts, and
resolve to follow the brethren,
those humble servants of that
great **Apostle** Who is the
elect representative
of the Father.

April 25

God
is Love
(1 John 4:8)

God is Love, and
His aether allows us to
catch a glimpse of heaven.
It permits us to bridge the
gulf between the tangible
world of everyday and
the anticipation of life
in celestial realms.

April 26

The Lamb Slain from Before the Foundation of the World
(Revelation 13:8)

Gethsemane was played out
at different times on many stages,
beginning before the earth's creation.
The Savior was **The Lamb Slain from
Before the Foundation of the World**.
His sacrifice will only end when the
last penitent sinner has stood with
courage before the bar of Justice
to receive intercession by the
Redeemer and forgiveness
from our Father, whose
outstretched arms
will encircle us
with His
love.

April 27

The Light, and the Life,
and the Truth
(Ether 4:12)

As sons
and daughters of
God, we are dedicated
to our duty and alive to our
opportunities. Because of our
faith and confidence in **The
Light, and the Life, and
the Truth**, we are not
susceptible to the
agitation that
leads to the
froth of
life.

April 28

The Lord of Heaven and Earth
(Matthew 11:25)

We are so short
sighted and self centered, boasting
of our accomplishments and our power,
seeking that which we can neither have nor hold;
never realizing that our might and strength,
and every faculty of our being are
gifts from Him Who is **The
Lord of Heaven
and Earth**.

April 29

The Lord God Almighty
(2 Nephi 28:15)

We have
never walked
alone, nor have we
faced our temptations in
solitude. We have never fought
our battles in weakness, nor have we
stood defenseless to face the enemy. **The
Lord God Almighty** is always with us.
His care envelops us, and His power
overcomes us. His mighty arm is
bared before our adversaries,
who shrink away before
His presence.

April 30

The
Living God
(Joshua 3:10)

We trust not
in stone nor in celluloid,
and neither in athletic prowess,
nor extraordinary physical attributes.
Not in power, position, wealth, or fame,
nor in political ideology, nor economic theory,
and not even in good health, or the wisdom
of age. Instead, we know to place our
confidence in **The Living God**, He
in Whom we live, and move,
and have our being.

May 1

Our Advocate with the Father
(1 John 2:1)

Spiritual Babylon measures our worth by its own corrupt standards, and reveres position, chattel, patronage, influence, and appearance. But **Our Advocate with the Father** searches instead the inner vessel, and seeks that which hands cannot hold and none may bestow upon us, even the sacrifice of our broken heart and contrite spirit. He measures us by putting the tape around our hearts, and not our heads. He gauges not the weight of our wallets, but the depth of our compassion.

May 2

The
Creator
(1 Peter 4:19)

He is the Maker of our being,
the Fashioner of our better nature,
the Influence behind our good deeds,
and **The Creator** of "all things bright and
beautiful, all creatures great and small,
all things wise and wonderful. The
Lord God made them all."
(Cecil Alexander).

May 3

The Lord your God
(Deuteronomy 10:17)

Thou
art the Holy
One of Israel and the
Savior of the world, and
I prostrate myself before Thee
and grow weak in Thy Presence as
I try to comprehend Thy power, might
majesty, and dominion. The Spirit speaks
so gently, whispering a quiet, yet powerful,
confirmation of the palpable stirrings
of religious recognition: **The Lord
your God** is Father of all.

May 4

The
Firstborn
(Romans 8:29)

In the
misty recesses
of our forgotten
memories, there stood
One above all. He was our
Elder Brother, **The Firstborn** in
the household of God. The sheep
of the fold know Him because
they recognize His familiar
voice, and are naturally
drawn to Him as
only next of
kin can
be.

May 5

The
Living Father
(John 6:57)

Too often,
the love of mammon
is at the very center of our
thoughts, capturing our attention,
and enticing us with its power, distorting
our vision, and warping our sense of reality.
It clutches us in its strong grip, tempting us
with subtlety, and in a fierce competition
with our better nature, it leaves soul
scars on our character that only
repentance can remove. **The
Living Father** helps us to
keep our focus on what
really matters.

May 6

Rabboni
(John 20:16)

Oh **Rabboni**, grant
us the power of discernment,
and watch over us. For scribes and
pharisees with golden tongues beguile
us with the wisdom of the world, tempt
us with sophistry, and drape flaxen
cords ever so gently around our
necks. It seems so reasonable
and so natural, even as we
are led ever so carefully
down to Hell.

May 7

The
Rock
(1 Samuel 2:2)

We should never allow
ouselves to get in the thick of
thin things, for there are only three
types of control in life. First, are things
over which we have direct control. Then,
there are circumstances over which we have
indirect control. Finally, are those situations over
which we have no control. In each of these settings,
it is **The Rock** Who is our Sure Foundation, and
the Anchor that grounds us to the bedrock
of the unchanging principles and
ordinances of His Gospel.

May 8

The Son
of the Eternal Father
(1 Nephi 13:40)

How
wonderful
it would be, if
it could be said of
each one of us that the
fabric of our character
contained not a single
shoddy thread, and
that we were one
with **The Son of
the Eternal
Father**.

May 9

(He) Who did no Sin
(1 Peter 2:22)

The Gospel
is our fortification,
and our obedience is our
best protection. He **Who did
no Sin** will shelter us from the
withering winds of wickedness
that are raking the land and
whipping up dust storms
of contention among
the people.

May 10

Jesus Christ
His Son
(1 John 1:7)

By doing our duty,
our faith increases until
it becomes perfect knowledge.
Can there be any difference, then,
between the two? Initially, faith is
simply to believe what we do not see,
and the reward of faith is to see what
we believe, to have the unspeakable
knowledge and assurance that
comes by the power of God
the Father and **Jesus
Christ His Son**.

May 11

Faithful and True
(Revelation 19:11)

Belief is simply
a mental assent to truth
without the moral element
of responsibility we call faith.
We believe that there is one God,
Who is **Faithful and True**, and
we do well. But "devils also
believe, and tremble."
(James 2:19).

May 12

The Head of the Church
(Ephesians 5:23)

The
bishop's miter, a
coveted red hat, and
robes of scarlet distract us
from the fact that no such
trappings were requried
by Him Who stands at
**The Head of the
Church.**

May 13

The Good Shepherd
(John 10:14)

As long as the Saints followed His teachings, the world was aflame with the fire of faith. Dark mists of apostasy dimmed the light, however, sowing discord and wickedness at every turn. After a long night, it has been within the crucible of the refiner's fire that the humble flock of **The Good Shepherd** has enjoyed a revelatory restoration of truth.

May 14

That Great Shepherd
of the Sheep
(Hebrews 13:20)

In the still
of the evening, when
darkness encroaches upon
us and we fear for our safety,
That Great Shepherd of the Sheep
will shelter us in His fold and
draw us close to His bosom.
He will bathe us in the
reassuring glow of
His inimitable
night light.

May 15

He that Came by Water and Blood
(1 John 5:6)

Ordinances
bind us to receive
Gospel blessings through
covenants of action, and bring us
to a more powerful understanding
of God's nature. **He that Came by Water and Blood** is also bound by
these authoritative covenants,
but when we do not what
He says, we have
no promise.

May 16

A High Priest
after the Order of Melchizedek
(Hebrews 5:10)

He
who
honors his
priesthood and
cherishes his family
will reap the blessings of
the celestial world. With the
**High Priest after the Order of
Melchizedek**, he will be a
father of many nations,
and a rightful
heir.

May 17

I am the Law
and the Light
(3 Nephi 15:9)

To follow
the Savior demands
active obedience to each
and every element of the Plan.
I am the Law and the Light gives
us assurance that a way will be
provided for us to comply
with all of the conditions,
terms, policies, notices,
features, and tools
relating to His
Gospel.

May 18

Jesus
(Romans 3:26)

He
was at
Ammonihah
when the walls fell,
and he comforted Nephi
on the seas. He labored with
the Sons of Mosiah among their
brethren the Lamanites, and when
the Title of Liberty was raised, He
stood with Moroni. **Jesus** will
always be beside us during
our moments of greatest
need.

May 19

The Lord God
of the Hebrews
(Exodus 7:16)

At times, we
feel like strangers in
a strange land, although
we are, in reality, a society of
Saints. Our Father, **The Lord
God of the Hebrews** succors
His people no matter where
they may have been
scattered over the
face of the
earth.

May 20

God
(Malachi 1:11)

It
is when
we are diligent
in our obedience to
the laws of the Gospel
that our agency enjoys its
greatest expression. That we
must yield ourselves to the
will of **God** is one of the
most difficult concepts
for the unconverted
to understand.

May 21

A Shadow of Heavenly Things
(Hebrews 8:5)

He is
A Shadow of Heavenly Things,
Who overcame the world with a message of peace. He taught that we may conquer our enemies, not with force, but through forgiveness.

May 22

(He Who) Put Away Sin
by the Sacrifice of Himself
(Hebrews 9:26)

He **Put
Away Sin by
the Sacrifice of Himself**.
The vivid imagery of the Savior
laboring under the weight of His cross
sears our individual and collective conscience.
Because we are also asked to carry very heavy
burdens, if we listen carefully, the Spirit
will quietly assure us that we will
never bear them alone.

May 23

The Rock of His Salvation
(Deuteronomy 32:15)

Zion stands
on principle, and
rededicates herself over altars
in the temple. She is anxious to be
taught, and learns with her heart. Zion
recognizes the glory of intelligence, light,
and truth, and is squarely founded on
the order of the priesthood. In Zion,
each inhabitant of the holy city
knows **The Rock of His
Salvation**.

May 24

The Savior
(Matthew 1:21)

Keeping our covenants with **The Savior** puts us beyond the reach of our adversaries. With our obedience, we are guaranteed the priesthood authority and spiritual power that are essential if we are to overcome the evil in the world and obtain exaltation.

May 25

The Shepherd of Israel
(Psalms 80:1)

As we make covenants, we soberly ponder a great truth: Knowledge endows us with responsibility. He who lived by both precept and by example, and Who was ever faithful to His calling, was **The Shepherd of Israel**.

May 26

The Shepherd and Bishop of your Souls
(1 Peter 2:25)

He is
the friend Who
will sacrifice for you, and
Who will never forsake you;
Who will leave the ninety and
nine to find you, and bring
you back into the fold.
He is **The Shepherd
and Bishop of
your Souls**.

May 27

The God of Abraham,
the God of Isaac,
the God of Jacob
(Exodus 3:6)

Our tithe
is but a token;
a tangible gesture
of our faith. For we
consecrate that which we
are. A greater offering is
found within our hearts.
Not just a tenth, but our
complete devotion to
the will of **The God
of Abraham, the
God of Isaac,**
and **the God
of Jacob**.

May 28

The
Faithful Witness
(Revelation 1:5)

Doubt
obscures the true
vision of our hearts.
The Faithful Witness of
Jesus Christ instead bears
an undeniable testimony
that replaces crippling
fear with saving faith
and infuses us with
His power.

May 29

A
Fellowservant
(Revelation 22:9)

Oh, that we
might be instruments
in Thy hands, and as Boanerges,
testify before the world of Thy love
for us, Thou **Fellowservant**! As Sons of
Thunder, give us strength to go into
Idumea to do Thy will, though
we may encounter giants
in the land!

May 30

The Glory of
the God of Israel
(Ezekiel 9:3)

My
Deliverer
and my Redeemer
is the Lord Who is **The
Glory of the God of Israel**.
In Him is my strength
and my salvation.

May 31

God
and His Father
(Revelation 1:6)

Elohim,
God and His Father,
preside over all their creations
and are co-eternal beings who dwell
in truth and light. They are the
same yesterday, today, and
forever. They exist in
harmony and unity
and are one with
each other.

June 1

God and the Father
(James 1:27)

We are born in His image and
likeness, and as we become older
we recapture the innocence of youth
by embracing the principles of the Plan
of our Father. We partake of His divine
nature. As we approach the character
of **God and the Father**, we join with
Them in a mystical union, until
we have become as one.

June 2

The God of
the Whole Earth
(Isaiah 54:5)

Some ask: Does
God know me, or is
He a respecter of persons?
Does He extend His love to me
unconditionally? Is He now here,
or is He nowhere? We know
that His family includes
all of His children, for
He is **The God of
the Whole
Earth**.

June 3

The Lord
of Lords
(1 Timothy 6:15)

The world
seeks to change
our behavior, while
the Master changes our
nature. Some actively seek
self-sufficiency, while others
yield themselves to Christ-
dependency. In the end,
He is **The Lord of
Lords**.

June 4

Christ
the Lamb
(Doctrine & Covenants 76:85)

The Saints cannot
hope to dwell in Zion
Estates, while at the same time
maintain expensive vacation retreats
on the sun kissed shores of Babylon Bay.
They cannot expect to joy-ride through Idumea,
stopping along the way to sample its pleasures.
They cannot, in one breath, acknowledge
Christ the Lamb, and with the next,
put Him to open shame with
casual remarks or with
careless behavior.

June 5

The Savior
of the Body
(Ephesians 5:23)

The Lord Jesus is
The Savior of the Body.
When reunited with our spirits,
our own resurrected bodies
will live as perfected souls
in His kingdom for
all eternity.

June 6

Him Which is, and Which was, and Which is to Come
(Revelation 1:8)

When we
choose to fill our
time and our space with
telestial toys whose opacity
makes it difficult to distinguish
between what is real and what is
an esoteric fancy, it is more difficult
to make room for **Him Which is,
and Which was, and Which
is to Come.**

June 7

The Spiritual Rock
(1 Corinthians 10:4)

When we
have enlisted in
the army of Israel,
we align ourselves with
The Spiritual Rock. We
stand with the priesthood
of God, gird ourselves in
robes of responsibility,
and listen carefully
for the call to
serve.

June 8

The
Spirit of Truth
(John 14:17)

Shall we
seek knowledge,
even hidden knowledge,
from The First Presidency and
Quorum of the Twelve, and search
the scriptures by **The Spirit of Truth**?
Surely, nothing shall escape our
attention, for the Lord shall
reveal His secret to the
prophets in the
Last Days.

June 9

Son Jesus Christ
our Lord
(1 John 5:20)

Our Father in
Heaven could very easily
give us everything He has, but
what He is, we must earn ourselves.
We work within His Plan of Happiness
to gain self-mastery on our way to
perfection, and look to His **Son
Jesus Christ our Lord** to
show us the way.

June 10

The Example
of the Son
(2 Nephi 31:16)

We
must obey the
commandment of
God to share the glad
tidings of joy, and warn
our neighbors. Inspired by
the Holy Ghost, we will follow
The Example of the Son and
teach the Gospel by the
spirit of truth.

June 11

Counselor
(2 Nephi 18:6)

Oh Lord,
we beg You to
minister to us in
Bethesda, when we
come to Thee in great
need. For when our
burdens are heavy,
we seek Thee as
our Counselor
in the holy
house of
God.

June 12

Jesus Christ
(Ephesians 2:20)

Faith in Jesus Christ that is coupled with our knowledge of the Plan of Salvation are co-equal driving forces propelling us along the pathway of eternal progress. We strive to gain mastery over the application of Gospel principles, because the Holy Spirit bears witness that therein lies the power to introduce us to eternal life in the kingdom of God.

June 13

(Him in Whom is) Eternal Life
(1 John 5:11)

There is an expanding
circle of opportunity afforded
by obedience to Gospel principles that
assures us of direct experience with Him
in Whom is **Eternal Life**. Our submission to
His will testifies that we have renounced the
uncertain course adopted by those bound
for a lesser kingdom, and have instead
embraced the certain expectation
of celestial glory.

June 14

The Lord
of the Whole Earth
(Doctrine & Covenants 55:1)

**The Lord
of the Whole Earth**
is in every sunrise and
sunset, in every flowering
shrub, and in every bird that
sings at the dawn of day. He
reveals Himself in a flowing
stream of love letters that
are heavily perfumed
with the scent of
spring.

June 15

The Lord God Omnipotent
(Mosiah 3:21)

Can it be possible that **The Lord God Omnipotent** shall speak, and His words be frustrated? Or shall He require justice, and not execute judgment? He has pronounced, and it is so. He has spoken, and His words are fulfilled.

June 16

The Son of the Living God
(Matthew 16:16)

We marvel at the ministry of our Lord and Savior, even as we recognize the remarkable certainty that He is **The Son of the Living God**, and has made a matchless sacrifice to save the world from sin.

June 17

The End of the Law for Righteousness
(Romans 10:4)

To the
world, we bear our
living witness of our Lord
Jesus Christ. Our testimonies
stand independently and require no
external warrant. At the Bar, we know
we shall all face our Maker. Our hope is that
when our lives are weighed in the balance,
the laws of Justice and Mercy will have
been forever reconciled through His
matchless intercession for His true
disciples. For them, He is **The
End of the Law for
Righteousness**.

June 18

The Shadow of Things to Come
(Colossians 2:17)

As our pre-mortal spiritual gestation period reached full term, we left the security of our celestial womb to come to earth through a portal of entry that is familiar to all. After a short interlude involving diaper changes and getting the hang of walking and talking, we are all destined to mature in ways that can be accomplished only by being clothed in mortal clay. At the time of our mission call, we engaged in an exit interview. He who was **The Shadow of Things to Come** explained how we would progress by both maturation and generation, and that we would grow to our full spiritual stature by being born not just once, but a second time to a newness of life that can only be found when we recognize the glory of our former home.

June 19

The Prophet
of the Highest
(Luke 1:76)

Our
prophets teach the
body of truth, and have
a certain witness of the Lord.
So too, when **The Prophet of
the Highest** reveals the
Plan of our Father, it
strikes a familiar
chord among
the sheep of
the fold.

June 20

The Holy One of Israel
(Psalms 89:18)

With the perspective that comes from enjoying a rapport with **The Holy One of Israel**, we come to a much clearer understanding of the dynamics of the spiritual foundations of interpersonal relationships. We seize upon the principle that all things have their opposites when we realize that the most powerful weapons against evil and darkness are truth and light.

June 21

The Lamb
that was Slain
(Revelation 5:12)

The Lamb that was Slain
is the perfect example of how
opposition can refine us. He was
born into a sinful world, and suffered
temptation as do we, but He led a perfect
life. He only asks us to repent with exactitude.
He has shown us how our nature can be pure and
undefiled, and how to build character that is flawless
and unimpeachable, through a spiritual rebirth. In
Gethsemane, before Pilate, during His scourging,
at Calvary, and finally before an empty tomb,
He showed us how to conquer death. He
now reigns in the heavens and waits
upon His Saints to trade telestial
uncertainties for celestial
sureties.

June 22

Father
(Acts 1:4)

The world is
transparent, and vanity
is evident everywhere we cast
our eyes. Commerce bustles about,
puffed up with self-importance. Should
we not instead be about our **Father's** business,
and devote our time and talents to endeavors
of a more enduring nature? The eternal
perspective of the Gospel endows us
with the power to move in the
direction of our dreams.

June 23

The Root of David
(Revelation 5:5)

In rich
and nurturing
Gospel soil, there
were sown the seeds
of righteousness. In the
beginning the Stem of Jesse,
we now know Him
as **The Root of
David**.

June 24

The Lord of the Vineyard
(Jacob 5:75)

From my small corner of the world, and from my narrow perspective of reality, I look out on the vast creations of God, and I begin to appreciate the mysterious truth that stirs my soul with religious recognition: He is **The Lord of the Vineyard**.

June 25

The Redeemer of the World
(Doctrine & Covenants 93:9)

Far too
often, we squander
our birthright for a mess
of pottage, as we enter into subtle
compacts with the devil. **The Redeemer
of the World** calls His disciples to embrace
a higher standard, where their word is as
solid as an oak, and where honesty and
integrity have been woven into the
very sinews of their being, for
all to see and to trust
implicitely.

June 26

Their Great and True Shepherd
(Helaman 15:13)

"'Tis not enough to help the feeble up, but to support him after." (Shakespeare, "Timon of Athens"). The weak and the frail know in Whom they may trust. They look up to **Their Great and True Shepherd**, Who lovingly tends to His flock, even after they have been gathered, with nurturing care.

June 27

God
our Savior
(Jude 1:25)

Thanks to
the intervention
of **God our Savior**, the
yoke of the faithful is easy,
and their burden is light.
Repentance removes the
taste of bitterness, and
leaves sweet savor
in its place.

June 28

(He Who) by Himself Purged our Sins
(Hebrews 1:3)

He Who
**by Himself
Purged our Sins**
has broken the barrier
of death, and offers the
hope of eternal life
to all who have
ever walked
over the
earth.

June 29

The Mediator
(1 Timothy 2:5)

When
I stand at
the Bar of Justice,
how can I adequately
defend myself? Without a
sinless **Mediator** to plead my
case with eloquence, and with
passion, power and authority,
not to mention legitimacy,
mine would be a
lost cause.

June 30

The
Rock of Heaven
(Moses 7:53)

During
the Great Council,
when our eternal destiny
hung in the balance, one voice
of reason united the better part of
the heavenly host, and rose clear
and resonant above the rest. He
was then, is now, and ever will
be, **The Rock of Heaven**, our
anchor, and the tangible
evidence of infinite
possiblities.

July 1

Offered Himself without Spot
(Hebrews 9:11)

Those who
cannot make the
vital distinction between
righteousness and wickedness
suffer eternally damaging consequences.
They are faced with a conundrum of cosmic
proportion, because they are free to follow
one lifestyle or the other, but not both.
That desire runs counter to the
laws of nature and to Him
Who **Offered Himself
without Spot**.

July 2

(He) Who was Foreordained Before the Foundation of the World
(1 Peter 1:20)

How can we
find real happiness? Neither
sickness nor health seems to holds the key.
Neither beauty nor the beast has an advantage.
Fame, anonymity, poverty and wealth have all failed.
Both principalities and the absence of worldly influence
are completely inadequate to accomplish the task.
Only He **Who was Foreordained Before
the Foundation of the World**
is able to help us.

July 3

The Fountain
of Living Waters
(Jeremiah 2:13)

Whenever I pause
in my persistent pursuit
of pleasure to drink deeply
from **The Fountain of Living
Waters**, I find refreshment as the
word of God revitalizes my soul in
a way that cannot be duplicated. I
realize that although river rafting
in the raging torrents that swirl
around me sounds exciting,
the experience can be life
threatening.

July 4

One Having Authority
(Matthew 7:29)

When
we are moved
upon to speak with
power in the Name of the
Lord, as **One Having
Authority**, miracles
are wrought in the
household of
faith.

July 5

The God of my Rock, my Shield, and the Horn
of my Salvation, my High Tower,
and my Refuge, my Savior
(2 Samuel 22:3)

He is **The God of my
Rock, my Shield, and the Horn
of my Salvation, my High Tower, and
my Refuge, my Savior**. He urged the man in
bondage to go the second mile, to lengthen his
stride, in order to remove the veil of insensitivity
to his destiny. When we are all wrapped up in
ourselves, we make very small packages.
Selfishness destroys moral fiber and
our ability to feel, while altruism
builds character and expands
our capacity to love.

July 6

The
King of Sion
(Matthew 21:5)

With a
mastery of the
equations that define
celestial principles, the citizens
of Zion are equipped to obey the law
of consecration. Their very nature is changed
and they become new creatures in Christ as they
righteously exercise the catalyzing influence of agency
in the biological broth of the laws and ordinances of
the Gospel. Within the petri dish of God's grand
experiment, their patron, **The King of Sion**,
infuses the inhabitants of the Holy City
with the nurturing culture medium
of faith and testimony.

July 7

Our Lord and Saviour
(2 Peter 3:2)

Among
all the sons
and daughters
of our Heavenly
Father, one stands
above all. In stature,
none are greater than
the Firstborn of every
creature, **Our Lord
and Saviour**.

July 8

The
Lamb
(Revelation 5:5)

Zion's
great mentor is
The Lamb. From Him,
she has learned to be meek
and patient, and she has charity
and hope. Because she has withdrawn
from the world's influence and shaken
free of the shackles of sin, she is able
to forge ahead and keep her eye
focused on an agenda that is
single to the glory
of God.

July 9

The
Most High God
(3 Nephi 11:17)

The
only motive
strong enough to
encourage us to exercise
the self-control requred by
The Most High God
is charity, or the
pure love of
Christ.

July 10

The Lord God
of Abraham
(Genesis 28:13)

**The Lord
God of Abraham**
stretches forth His arm,
and it is mighty to save. As rolling
thunder, His voice is heard above the
tumult of opinion. As a rushing of waters,
His word is revealed. His face is as lightning,
and His tongue like a two-edged sword,
to divide asunder both joint and
marrow, and to lay bare
the spirit.

July 11

The Seed
of Abraham
(Galatians 3:16)

"The
universe is but
one great city, full of
beloved ones, human and
divine, by nature endeared
to each other." (Epictetus).
Within its warm embrace,
all are one with **The
Seed of Abraham**.

July 12

Messias
(John 4:25)

Happy
are the Saints who
assemble together in their
synagogues, there to enjoy the
companionship of the faithful, and
to worship **Messias**, the Anointed
One. They shall bear each other
up upon the wings of eagles,
and their congregations
shall resonate with the
joyful melodies of
anticipation.

July 13

The
Stone of Israel
(Doctrine & Covenants 50:44)

A house
divided against
itself cannot stand. The
Church of **The Stone of Israel**
has again been established on the
earth, and it will not compromise
its standards in order to become
popular with the world, for
then all hell would want
to join with it.

July 14

The Way, the Truth, and the Life
(John 14:6)

When my vision is
blurred by distractions,
and I wander from the path
that would lead me home, my
compass puts me back on course.
The Way, the Truth, and the Life,
my Liahona, guides me unerringly,
on to my eternal destiny. Without
it, my progress would falter
and I would be lost.

July 15

(He) Who Knew no Sin
(2 Corinthians 5:21)

He Who Knew no Sin was tempted above that which others could have endured. He triumphed over every test of character and descended beneath us all in order to fulfil His holy calling as our Redeemer.

July 16

The
Lord is the
Strength of my Life
(Psalms 27:1)

**The Lord
is the Strength
of my Life.** He is the
rudder of my ship, my
helm, my telltale, my keel,
my mainsheet, my compass,
my chart, my barometer, my
sextant, and my lookout.
He is the wind that
fills my sails.

July 17

Lord our Righteousness
(Jeremiah 23:6)

There is no
file corruption in the
Lord our Righteousness. His
data storage capacity is infinite.
No virus threatens the integrity of
His program. Every necessary firewall
has been downloaded and installed
to protect His users from hackers.
As they look to His screen for
guidance, they are met by a
reassuring smiling face.
No frown.

July 18

(He who is) Made Higher than the Heavens
(Hebrews 7:26)

Zion
comprehends
with wide-eyed wonder,
and in deference to her great
Mentor, He Who is **Made Higher
than the Heavens**, removes her shoes
from off her feet. She knows when
she is in the presence of a
burning bush that is
not consumed.

July 19

Emmanuel
(Matthew 1:23)

Father,
grant us a safe
haven from the world
at Bethel, the home of
Emmanuel. It is in
the house of God
that we will find
our rest and
sanctuary.

July 20

The Foundation of the Church
(1 Corinthians 3:11)

Those
who camp out at
the base of Mount Sinai,
wait for a prophet to bring
a law of carnal commandments.
How much better it would be
if only they could raise their
sights, and focus upon the
greater law of **The
Foundation of
the Church**.

July 21

God our Father
and the Lord Jesus Christ
(Romans 1:7)

As the morning
breaks over the eastern sky,
with theatrical encore the sunrise
heralds another day. Once more, the
self-evident question is raised: Will you
choose today whom you will serve?
Answer, then, with conviction. We
will follow **God our Father and
the Lord Jesus Christ**.

July 22

(He in Whom is) Salvation
(2 Timothy 2:10)

He in Whom is **Salvation**
will save us by His matchless grace
that consists of the gifts and powers of
heaven by which we may be brought to
His perfection, in an expansion of our
potential that allows us to enjoy
not only what He has, but
also what He is.

July 23

(Him Who) hath Perfected Forever
them that are Sanctified
(Hebrews 10:14)

Lord, we pray
that we might not be
indifferent disciples; that our
devotions might be profound;
that we might bring forth Zion,
and be called by that name most
dear and familiar to us: Latter-
day Saints; members of the
Church of Him Who **hath
Perfected Forever
them that are
Sanctified**.

July 24

Lord
even of the Sabbath
(Matthew 12:8)

We awaken to a beautiful Sunday morning, and as we consider the day that lies ahead, we remember that the Son of Man is **Lord even of the Sabbath**, and that we are His servants. We are charged with the responsibility to care for part of His vineyard. Our resolve to be profitable stewards is energized by that sobering realization.

July 25

A
Branch
(Isaiah 11:1)

Those who
accept neither the
Gospel, nor the authority
of the priesthood, will be left
with neither root nor branch. That
is to say, in the resurrection of the just
they will have neither forebearers nor
posterity, because they have rejected
the sealing ordinances. For them, it
will be as if the **Branch**, that was
once so vibrant and full of life,
has withered and died
in vain.

July 26

The
King of Kings
(Revelation 17:14)

He was
King of Kings,
but never traveled
far from home. He had
few material possessions
and rode into Jerusalem on
the back of another's donkey.
He suffered the indignity of the
pretense of a trial, and was crucified
with common thieves. Then, His body
was taken to a borrowed tomb. But
what He did then, no other king
had ever done before, nor has
since. His majesty is
unparalleled.

July 27

The Governor that Shall Rule Israel
(Matthew 2:6)

"He who shall introduce into public affairs the principles of primitive Christianity will revolutionize the world." (Benjamin Franklin). He who does so, follows the matchless example of **The Governor that Shall Rule Israel**.

July 28

Alpha and Omega
(Revelation 1:11)

There
is nothing
our Lord does not
know, for He is **Alpha
and Omega**, the Beginning
and the End, and His eye
pierceth all things. To
Him, our hearts
and our minds
are as open
books.

July 29

The God
of thy Father
(Genesis 46:3)

There are some who believe
that we are made of stardust, and will
one day return from whence we came; that
we are the offspring of supernovae; that they
created us and are responsible for everything we
see. They would have us believe that the destiny of
the universe lies in the ashes of dying stars. Perhaps,
after all is said and done, it is to the heavens that we
should turn to see where creation and destriction
meet. **The God of thy Father** teaches an even
greater truth: We came from our heavenly
home trailing clouds of glory, and will
one day return amidst the fire and
smoke of celestial, and not
telestial or terrestrial,
burnings.

July 30

The King
of all the Earth
(Psalms 47:7)

You will
never discover
new oceans without
mustering the courage to
lose sight of the shore from
whence you came. And so, we
trust **The King of all the Earth**,
Who rules on the both land and
the sea, and in the starry sky,
and Who commands the
elements, and they
obey.

July 31

A Lamb without Blemish and without Spot
(1 Peter 1:19)

What
sacrifice is too great?
Or to whom should we turn to
provide the pre-eminent example? To
the **Lamb without Blemish and without Spot**,
Who, without hesitation, prostrated Himself
on the greatest altar of all, and said:
"Thy will be done."

August 1

The Living God and an Everlasting King
(Jeremiah 10:10)

We begin to understand something of the physical and spiritual rapport that exists between our Heavenly Father and His Son Jesus Christ, when we feel a similar connection between Them and ourselves. As the Holy Ghost facilitates this mystical union, we become one in a spiritual sense with Him Who is **The Living God and an Everlasting King**.

August 2

A
Stone
(Jacob 4:15)

He is
A Stone,
our Anchor to
the infinite, our
Sure Foundation, a
Precious Jewel mined
from a celestial
quarry.

August 3

The Judge of Both the Quick and the Dead
(Acts 10:42)

He is **The Judge of Both the Quick and the Dead**. All must submit to baptism as a token of obedience; not only the living, but also those who have passed on. For the holy scriptures plainly teach that "except a man be born of water and of the Spirit, he cannot enter into the kingdom of God." (John 3:5).

August 4

The Light of Israel
(2 Nephi 20:17)

As we prostrate ourselves before **The Light of Israel**, we are humbled by the awful tokens of His sacrifice in His hands, His side, and His feet. We resolve with greater determination to make sure that His suffering was not in vain.

August 5

The Son
of the Highest
(Luke 1:32)

Our
journey to
the Mountain
of the Lord's House
takes us no further than
to the temple, where **The
Son of the Highest** abides,
and the Spirit is able to
speak peace to
our souls.

August 6

Our
Passover
(Hebrews 13:1)

His
mighty hand
will rule in the Last
Days, and His people
have no need to fear the
awful threats and vile oaths
of the wicked. Even when
the Angel of Death is
abroad in the land,
the Lord is **Our
Passover**.

August 7

The Mighty God of Jacob
(Psalms 132:2)

Our Deliverer is **The Mighty God of Jacob**. He fulfills all His words, and blesses those who love Him. Yea, the righteous shall fall at His feet, and with tears of joy accept His counsel. Then, on wings of glory shall they ascend into heaven to be with Him.

August 8

The Mediator of a Better Covenant
(Hebrews 8:6)

**The
Mediator of
a Better Covenant**
raised the bar when He set
a standard of behavior for His
chosen people. As a brazen serpent,
He was lifted up so that His power
could draw us to Him, setting
us free to commence our
own beginning and
becoming.

August 9

Almighty
(Revelation 1:8)

The
Almighty
is our strength
and our salvation
Who stretches out
His arm to bring
us into His
Rest.

August 10

(He Who is) Better than the Angels
(Hebrews 1:4)

Abiding
in a realm of light
among perfected and
exalted beings, He Who is
Better than the Angels brings
order to each of His creations,
extending His influence
even to the least
of us.

August 11

There is One God, and One Mediator
between God and Men, the Man Christ Jesus
(1 Timothy 2:5)

Being His
disciple has less
to do with fitting a mold
that others have created for us,
and more to do with knowing and
pleasing our Savior by pursuing a standard
of behavior that fills the measure of our creation.
In our minds, one certainty always stands out:
**There is One God, and One Mediator
between God and Men, the Man
Christ Jesus.**

August 12

The
Lord God
(Jude 1:4)

We hear the
voice of **The Lord God**
when thunder rolls, lightning
streaks, or clouds scud across windswept
skies. His speech is recorded in the profusion
of wildflowers strewn over the fields and
meadows of early spring. Surely, "the
heavens declare the glory of God,
and the firmament sheweth
his handiwork."
(Psalms 19:1).

August 13

The
Forerunner
(Hebrews 6:20)

The Forerunner
goes first, setting the
pace for the entire race, noting
obstacles, and identifying pitfalls.
Then, it is our turn, and though "the
stars fade away, the sun himself grow dim
with age, and nature sink in years, we shall
flourish in immortal youth, unhurt amidst the
war of elements, the wreck of matter, and the
crash of worlds." (Joseph Addision, "Cato").

August 14

The Living Bread
which Came down from Heaven
(John 6:51)

Our
burning
thirst is only
quenched by healing
water, and so the purging
of our corruption begins as we
drink deeply from its quickening
currents. So too, we can also avoid
certain spiritual starvation as we
partake of **The Living Bread
which Came down from
Heaven**, and enjoy
it as our daily
fare.

August 15

The Witness of God
(1 John 5:9)

The Witness of God speaks peace to our souls, through a testimony of His divinity that is borne by the Spirit.

August 16

A Teacher Come From God
(John 3:2)

We
need a
great mentor,
even **A Teacher
Come from God**,
because we are all
travelers who are
simply exploring
both the byways
and highways
of mortality
for the first
time.

August 17

(He Who made) Angels, Authorities, and Powers…Subject to Him
(1 Peter 3:22)

He Who made **Angels, Authorities, and Powers Subject to Him** inspired the poet who gave voice to the guiding principle: "To thine own self be true!" (Shakespeare).

August 18

The Holy One,
the Creator of Israel
(Isaiah 43:15)

The Holy One, the Creator of Israel, has a simple but unmistakable mission statement: To bring to pass our immortality and eternal life. "The universe," after all, "is a machine for the making of Gods." (Henri Bergson).

August 19

God and Father of our Lord Jesus Christ
(1 Peter 1:3)

Our joy is full, and so with gladness we lift up our eyes to gaze upon heaven. The horizon of our vision is eternal, and through the parted veil we can almost hear angelic voices crying Hosanna, in praise of the **God and Father of our Lord Jesus Christ**.

August 20

(Him Who) hath Given us an Understanding that we may Know Him that is True
(1 John 5:20)

"Understanding is the reward of faith. Therefore, seek not to understand, that thou mayest believe, but believe, that thou mayest understand." (St. Augustine). Trust that you might draw near to **Him Who hath Given us an Understanding that we may Know Him that is True**.

August 21

The
Almighty God
(Genesis 17:1)

When
taunted by
Babylon, we
declare ourselves
for the Lord Who is
The Almighty God.
Amid swirling mists
of gloom, we hold
fast to the Rod of
Iron that is His
Word.

August 22

The
Great Creator
(Jacob 3:7)

As we
stand in awe of
our surroundings, trying
to make sense of our place in
the cosmos, a voice quietly whispers
to us, assuring us of our heavenly lineage.
So full of hope and promise, it speaks peace
to our souls, as we contemplate the
magnificent work and glory
of **The Great Creator**.

August 23

The Lord Jehovah
(Isaiah 12:2)

Those who have been living under the bondage of sin may one day be blessed with a sudden sunburst of spiritual sensitivity. When this epiphany comes, they may realize for the first time that it is **The** mighty **Lord Jehovah** Who, all along, has been quietly choreographing their lives. As they begin to appreciate that it is He Who governs their affairs and is the true Light of the World, they will require the sustaining support of a sympathetic priesthood that ministers to their developing needs, so that they may continue to be astonished, but never blinded, by the brilliance of His presence, the power of His doctrine, or the demands of His discipleship.

August 24

Lord the King of Israel
(Isaiah 44:6)

Before her
enemies, Zion unfurls
her terrible banners, and
stands fast in the name of the
powerful **Lord the King of Israel**.
She does not engage in popularity
contests with the world, does not
seek its approval, nor will she
compromise her standards,
settle for mediocre effort,
or engage in negotiation
in order to achieve a
conciliation with
Babylon.

August 25

The God
of the Hebrews
(Exodus 5:3)

We
are Israelites
whether by blood
or by adoption, and
we claim the blessings
of our father Abraham,
and Isaac, and Jacob.
With **The God of
The Hebrews**
we have cast
our lot.

August 26

The Seed of David
(2 Timothy 2:8)

"The mystic bond of brotherhood makes all men one." (Thomas Carlyle). Christ was **The Seed of David**, and we are heirs of His covenant made with Abraham that joins us together in an unshakable spiritual union.

August 27

The Author
of Eternal Salvation
(Hebrews 5:9)

If our
testimonies
begin to wobble
and shake, we need to
remember that the quarry
from which they spring is a
source of stability, for it provides
the stone with which we may build
a solid and enduring foundation.
Our faltering faith will always
find steadiness in **The
Author of Eternal
Salvation**.

August 28

The Lord,
for He is our God
(Joshua 24:18)

He was
the innocent Lamb
Whose sacrifice was infinite
in nature and eternal in scope;
an unfathomable offering.
He is **The Lord, for He
is our God**.

August 29

A
Refiner's Fire
(Malachi 3:2)

Our
ordeals are
as a fuller's soap
and **A Refiner's Fire**.
At first, we may shrink
from the bitter cup. But
then, we will endure, and
finally come to embrace
what are really golden
opportunities for
growth and
renewal.

August 30

Lord God
of your Fathers
(Deuteronomy 1:11)

I would like
to know Him better, to
return to the comfort and security
of His enveloping care, to enjoy His
sweet companionship, and to love Him
more profoundly. I want to come back to
the familiar surroundings of my former
home. For now, I will content myself
to sit at the feet of His prophets,
who testify to me: He is the
**Lord God of your
Fathers**.

August 31

The Mediator of
the New Testament
(Hebrews 9:15)

Zion
emulates
the holiness of
**The Mediator of
the New Testament**.
Her power to do so is
the result of a spiritual
transformation that
has come about as
she lives His
celestial
law.

September 1

Christ Jesus
(Romans 3:24)

It is
a time for
choosing **Christ
Jesus** or the adversary.
For peace has been taken
from the earth, and the devil,
who has power over his
own dominion, seeks
to control our
lives, as
well.

September 2

Captain
(2 Chronicles 13:12)

He could easily
provide us with what
He has, for He is our **Captain**,
and the earth and the seas are His
dominion. But what He is, He cannot
summarily give us, for it must be earned.
The Gospel is a training vessel that has been
designed with one purpose only in mind, and
that is to carry us past reefs and shoals while
teaching us the skills and providing us with
the resources that are necessary to chart a
course through the eternities that will
unerringly guide us back to the
safe haven of our heavenly
home.

September 3

(He Who is) Crowned with Glory and Honour
(Hebrews 2:9)

He Who is
**Crowned with Glory
and Honour** taught that the
best things in life aren't things,
and that our temporal treasures
can leave soul-scars that only
the process of repentance
can remove.

September 4

(Him Who hath) Obtained Eternal Redemption For Us
(Hebrews 9:12)

The discrepancy
between Gospel ideals
and the behavior of the wicked
will become obvious even to them, as
they gain knowledge and understanding.
The short-lived pleasure they have taken
in sin will evaporate as a mist in the
heat of the day. Then will come a
difficult reconciliation with Him
Who hath **Obtained Eternal
Redemption For Us**.

September 5

The
Blessed of God
(Psalms 45:2)

Hope
that is born
of faith gives us
the assurance of peace,
that in spite of the turmoil
that surrounds us, our lives
can be oriented along a course
that leads to eternal life, and
that the gifts and favors of
The Blessed of God may
rest upon our heads
to consecrate our
efforts.

September 6

The Minister of the Sanctuary and of the True Tabernacle
(Hebrews 8:2)

His
habitation
is our refuge and
the horns of mercy our
salvation. We take them in
our grasp, and dare not let go,
secure in the knowledge that
He is **The Minister of the
Sanctuary and of the
True Tabernacle**.

September 7

Our
Lawgiver
(Isaiah 33:22)

Torah has
been engraven upon
our hearts and guides our
actions. Without conscious effort,
we hold fast to that which is true. By
the power of the Holy Ghost, we are
given wisdom. For **Our Lawgiver**
has stitched understanding into
our sinews and into the very
fabric of our being.

September 8

Our
Heavenly King
(Mosiah 2:19)

**Our
Heavenly King**
determines how much we
must pay to live in the best part
of town, in His neighborhood, in the
home of our dreams, within the sphere
of His protective influence. It is simply our
submission to His will. We are on probation,
so the cost is built into a lease, which can be
voided if we choose to do so. But He has
provided a generous purchase option
that allows us to apply every one of
the payments we have already
made through obedience, to
the listed asking price of
eternal life.

September 9

The Prince of the Kings of the Earth
(Revelation 1:5)

"How carefully most men creep into nameless graves, while now and again one or two forget themselves into immortality." (Phillips Brooks). **The Prince of the Kings of the Earth** set the example for us to follow, for He was the servant of all.

September 10

(Him) in Whom are Hid all the Treasures of Wisdom and Knowledge
(Colossians 2:3)

The power to
convey the application of
eternal principles comes through
the Spirit that resides in Him **in Whom are Hid all the Treasures of Wisdom and Knowledge**. He is our mentor who delivers the word, and we are the students who are its grateful recipients. We are quickened by the influence of His inspiration. This is the enchantment of our Gospel instruction.

September 11

The High Calling of God
(Philippians 3:14)

"My life is my message." (Gandhi). We are all enlightened by **The High Calling of God**. But every now and then, He sends a shooting star to appear in the heavens and inspire us. These men and women testify by their actions that guiding principles can be points of light with which we take our bearings on eternity.

September 12

I
Am
(John 8:58)

Time is
not the heartless
taskmaster that some think
it to be. It is, rather, a perceptive
companion that quietly provides the
fabric upon which we stitch our
cherished memories. **I Am** is
ever before us, however, to
remind us that we are
immortal.

September 13

One
with the Father
(John 10:30)

At
their baptisms,
unity and completion
describe the faithful, who
are **One with the Father**, and "are
no more strangers and foreigners, but
(are) fellowcitizens with the saints,
and of the household of God."
(Ephesians 2:19).

September 14

Their Rock
and their Salvation
(1 Nephi 15:15)

We
who first
lived with God
received wise counsel
before leaving our first estate:
"I could so easily give you what I have,
but what I am, you must earn for yourself."
Obedience to the principles of the Plan will guide
our steps, and following the graduation ceremonies
that mark the completion of our second estate
curriculum, the faithful will enjoy a home-
coming celebration back in the presence
of **Their Rock and their Salvation**.

September 15

(He Who) hath an Unchangeable Priesthood
(Hebrews 7:24)

He Who **hath an Unchangeable Priesthood** delegates to others His authority to minister in our affairs. He rarely intervenes directly, but rather gives assignments to His servants, and then makes it possible for them to accomplish the work.

September 16

An Offering and Sacrifice to God
(Ephesians 5:2)

In the Last Days, discipleship will be lived in crescendo, as the Gospel standard is ever more sharply contrasted with the shifting sands of the world's values. The resulting polarity only highlights the behavior of those who are true to their covenants and have made **An Offering and Sacrifice to God**.

September 17

Maker
(Hosea 8:14)

There
is one word
that describes the
Builder of all things, the
Author of eternal salvation,
and the Creator of numberless
worlds. He is the Master of
the universe. He is our
Maker.

September 18

Merciful
(2 Chronicles 30:9)

It is
by His design
that we learn from our
mistakes and our trespasses.
He knew that our experiences would
have a dark side, and that evil influences
would jostle for our attention. So, we do
everything that lies within our power to
obtain the favor of a **Merciful** God,
even as we carefully pick our
way through the minefields
of mortality.

September 19

The
Lord of Hosts
(Isaiah 5:16)

Of whom
will we sing praises, and
to whom will we shout Hosanna?
The Lord of Hosts is our Redeemer.
Our Savior is the Great Jehovah.
Surely God will save now,
and we will honor His
name forever.

September 20

Our
Deliverer
(Romans 11:16)

The Lord
is **Our Deliverer**
Whose teachings provide
the solutions to our problems.
There must be a special place in His
heart for those who love Him. These
are the righteous and true, who shall
fall before Him, wash His feet with
their tears, and joyfully accept His
inspired counsel. On wings of
glory they shall ascend into
heaven to be near Him.

September 21

The Apostle and High Priest of our Profession
(Hebrews 3:1)

The great destroyer is abroad in the land, and the world dances to the siren song of Babylon that rings so seductively and persistently in its ears. God grant us protection from these influences, and from that crafty old serpent Beelzebub. We must not fail Him Who is **The Apostle and High Priest of our Profession**.

September 22

A Light to Lighten the Gentiles
(Luke 2:32)

The Savior Jesus Christ is **A Light to Lighten the Gentiles**, and a dazzling gift from Heavenly Father to all the sheep who are not of the fold. As the Gospel goes into all the world, there is awakened even in them the spark of divinity.

September 23

Our
Redeemer
(Isaiah 59:20)

For scientific discovery, we turn to the intellect of those within the ivory towers of academia, and the images of those with speed and athletic prowess adorn the walls of our various halls of fame. But when disaster strikes, and all hope of rescue has vanished, and stirrings of panic begin to rise in our gut, we get down on our knees and cry out to **Our Redeemer** for the help that only He can provide.

September 24

The Propitiation for the Sins of the Whole World
(1 John 2:2)

Christ was the **Propitiation for the Sins of the Whole World**. The cleansing waters of baptism extend an invitation to the penitent, the modest, the meek and lowly, the poor in spirit, and the pure in heart, to come unto Him. He taught: "Strait is the gate, and narrow is the way, which leadeth unto life, and few there be that find it." (Matthew 7:14). We are humbled to count ourselves among the fortunate few, and we promise to be persistent as we perform to the potential of our privileged position.

September 25

The Son of the Blessed
(Mark 14:61)

In His form, He is in the express image of God, for He is **The Son of the Blessed**. He is of royal lineage and is a rightful heir of every good thing that has been promised by His Father in Heaven.

September 26

The God over all the Earth
(1 Nephi 11:6)

The God over all the Earth is in every sunrise and in every sunset; in every flowering shrub, and every bird that sings at the dawn of every day. He manifests Himself to us in an endless stream of love letters. "Earth is crammed with heaven, and every common bush with fire of God. But only those who see, take off their shoes. The rest stand around picking blackberries." (E.B. Browning).

September 27

Our
Shield
(Genesis 15:1)

The word
of the Lord is an
ensign to the nations and
His standard is ever before us
He is **Our Shield** for a defense.
His voice is as a two-edged
sword. In His scriptures,
we shall find solace,
for the Rod of Iron
clearly defines
our path.

September 28

The
Holiest of All
(Hebrews 9:3)

Today, we can try to do better.
Today, we can give a tithe of our time.
Today, we can walk where Jesus walked.
Today, we can minister to the needs of others.
Today, we can partake of the emblems of His sacrifice.
Today, we can teach another the principles of His Gospel.
Today, we can feel the love and the presence of
Him Who is **The Holiest of All**.

September 29

The Creator of Heaven and Earth
(Jacob 2:5)

God
pronounced all
things good that He
had made with His hands.
Then, He entrusted it all into
our care, to be nurtured and
safeguarded. For it is the
handiwork of Him who
is **The Creator of
Heaven and
Earth**.

September 30

The Rock
of my Strength
(Isaiah 17:10)

My wounds make me wince with pain, and my suffering seems greater than I can bear. Yet my body and spirit, my very soul, can be at peace, and my anxieties can dissolve, when I allow myself to fall under the influence of **The Rock of my Strength**.

October 1

Blessed for Evermore
(2 Corinthians 11:31)

When the Spirit helps us to understand the nature of God our Father, we are poised to embark upon a voyage of discovery leading to Him Who is **Blessed for Evermore**.

October 2

A High Priest of Good Things to Come
(Hebrews 9:11)

For many,
life is a journey
whose destination
is uncertain. They fear
death as an "undiscovered
country from whose bourne no
traveler returns." (Shakespeare,
"Hamlet"). The Saints, however,
take comfort in their unbridled
confidence in the One Who
is **A High Priest of Good
Things to Come**.

October 3

Christ
of God
(John 9:20)

Our abilities merge with
His power when we are reconciled
to **Christ of God**. Focusing that energy
on our faith vitalizes belief that can become
a catalyst that motivates us to action that
leads to higher levels of achievement.
Perhaps this is why we intuitively
know that if our faith lacks
works, it is of no value.
It is dead, being
alone.

October 4

Jehovah, Mighty God of Jacob
(Doctrine & Covenants 109:68)

Our incomprehensible debt to Jehovah, the **Mighty God of Jacob,** is totally beyond our ability to pay. There is nothing that we can do that obligates Him to us. But He doesn't ask us to settle our account with Him. He only asks that we keep His commandments. The marvel of His great love for us is that the more we serve Him, the more He blesses us. We become even more deeply indebted, and remain so forever. We are bound to Him through love.

October 5

The
Lord of All
(Acts 10:36)

Jesus Christ
is **The Lord of All**.
He "denieth none that
come unto him, black and
white, bond and free, male and
female; and he remembereth
the heathen, and all are
alike unto God, both
Jew and Gentile."
(2 Nephi 26:33).

October 6

The Highest of All
(Doctrine & Covenants 76:70)

With
all of Israel,
we raise our voices.
He is **The Highest of All**,
and we are His Chosen
People. We sense
acceptance from
Him Who
matters
most.

October 7

Jesus Christ, the Son of God,
the Father of Heaven and Earth,
the Creator of all Things
From the Beginning
(Mosiah 3:8)

We are
Born Again
with the promise of
unexpected opportunity
and unlimited possibility, and
the rebirth charges us with excitement
and anticipation. We have the confidence
that comes through covenants made
with **Jesus Christ, the Son of God,
the Father of Heaven and Earth,
the Creator of all Things
From the Beginning**.

October 8

The Hope
of His People
(Joel 3:16)

"He that hath
seen me hath seen the
Father." (John 14:9). Jesus
has revealed Himself to Israel as
The Hope of His People. It is within
the nature of the Savior that the children
of the covenant are able to discover
the character of God.

October 9

The Mediator of the New Covenant
(Hebrews 12:24)

Ever
before us is
**The Mediator of
the New Covenant**, and
Abraham is its rightful heir.
Whether by blood or adoption,
we are of the lineage of the Father
of the Faithful, and shall enjoy
all of the blessings that have
been promised to him
and his righteous
seed.

October 10

The Messenger of the Covenant
(Malachi 3:1)

In the Last Days, the Saints will be moved to exclaim: Hallelujah. Before the Millennial Day, when the sign of the Lord is near, and **The Messenger of The Covenant** is poised in the clouds to reclaim His kingdom, they shall cry out: "Praise ye the Lord!"

October 11

One Eternal God
(Alma 11:44)

The members of the Godhead are one in purpose, and are completely unified, thinking alike, and acting in harmony, as **One Eternal God**.

October 12

Shiloh
(Ezekiel 21:27)

When our priorities are in order, me and mine yield to thee and thine. Ultimately, we look to **Shiloh**, He to Whom it Belongs, for our sum and substance.

October 13

Lord
(Matthew 28:6)

I will delight in the
commandments of the **Lord**, for
they are a great blessing to the faithful.
He prospers those who keep His
word, and honors those who
love to obey His voice.

October 14

The
Prince of Peace
(Isaiah 9:6)

**The Prince
of Peace** stands
unruffled and serene
in a world turned upside
down by telestial turmoil, sensory
overload, and every tumult of opinion.
Carnal confusion, conceptual cul-de-sacs,
discord, unrest, and a war of words
are eradicated by Him Who is
our stronghold of stability
and tranquility.

October 15

The Head Stone of the Corner
(Psalms 118:22)

We are the agents
of our destiny and the
architects of our own fate,
and our labor correctly applied
will see the building fitly framed.
But beyond our own efforts, a greater
power is at work. Our Redeemer, Who
is **The Head Stone of the Corner**, serves
as our General Contractor and oversees
our efforts. Although He will sub out
much of the work, ultimately it is
by Him alone that an extreme
home makeover transforms
our poor habitations into
royal mansions.

October 16

The Very Eternal Father of Heaven and of Earth
(Alma 11:39)

It was not just a
gathering for supper with
devoted disciples, and was more
than transubstantiated flesh and blood.
Bread and water became symbols,
tokens of our covenant with
**The Very Eternal Father
of Heaven and
of Earth.**

October 17

Jehovah
(Exodus 6:3)

Shall the Lord
remember His children,
and keep the covenant He has
made with them? Or shall He defend
Zion with His outstretched arm, and go before
His army with terrible banners? We know in our
hearts that **Jehovah** saves and remembers His
promises to the faithful. He is a Refuge to
His little ones, and has promised to lead
Israel to a fruitful land flowing with
milk and honey.

October 18

An Everlasting Light
(Isaiah 60:19)

When we are baptized, we make a statement. Then, when we receive the Holy Ghost, the Lord makes His own unequivocal statement. He becomes **An Everlasting Light** to banish the darkness from our lives with the power of the Spirit.

October 19

The Law
and the Light
(3 Nephi 15:9)

So that we might avoid
a catastrophic conundrum with
cosmic consequences, agency has been
preserved as mortality's crown jewel.
We are free to choose, but choose
we must. It is from **The Law
and the Light** that we are
given both the principles
and the inspiration to
wisely exercise our
free will.

October 20

The Holy One and the Just
(Acts 3:14)

When in close proximity to spiritual experiences, the unrepentant feel uncomfortable and uneasy with **The Holy One and the Just**, and they withdraw to lifestyles devoid of His companionship. Thus begins a solitary downward spiral that gains momentum as sinful behavior is more easily committed and becomes entrenched.

October 21

The Door of the Sheep
(John 10:7)

Jesus
is **The Door
of the Sheep** who
hears our prayers in those
sacred moments when we bond
with the Spirit of God. As we do so,
we are touching His garment. At the
same time, He can feel virtue flow
from Him. At that moment, we
discover something that He
has always known: He
is forever within
our reach.

October 22

The First Begotten of the Dead
(Revelation 1:5)

In the
Merciful Plan
of our Father, we
were ordained to come
into this world to die. When
he was placed in the Garden, it
was clearly explained to Adam that
his transgression of God's law would
trigger mortality. **The First Begotten
of the Dead** is proof of His inspired
preparation for that eventuality,
and for both the redemption
and the resurrection of the
posterity of Adam
and Eve.

October 23

The Law, and the Life, and the Truth
(Ether 4:12)

When we turn
our faces to the Son, we are
comforted by His warm embrace.
The Law, and the Life, and the Truth
encourages us onward, and makes sure
that the shadows are always behind us.
We are born not only of blood or water,
but also of Spirit, in celestial realms.
We know we are of a royal lineage,
and instinctively yield ourselves
to the better angels of
our nature.

October 24

The Captain
of our Salvation
(Hebrews 2:10)

The Captain of our Salvation honors the principle of free will that reigns supreme in the universe. In essence, He says: "I could give you what I have, but what I am, you must earn for yourself. My Gospel is a schoolmaster to bring you to me. Then, all that is within My Kingdom shall be yours."

October 25

Author
(Moroni 6:4)

The debate is
clearly over when
the **Author** of Salvation
has spoken. Our promises
to Him are binding contracts,
and since He is a party to each
and every covenant, they must
come directly from His throne
by revelation. The only ones
who can reasonably enter
into these covenants are
those of His Church
who believe that
He still speaks
to us.

October 26

(He Who was)
Sent that we might Live
through Him
(1 John 4:9)

How
comforting it is
to know that when life
throws us a curve, as it does
with frustrating but inevitable
regularity, our disappointment and
discouragement can be conquered
by faith and our trust in the one
Eternal Optimist, He Who was
**Sent that we might Live
through Him.**

October 27

Joseph's Son
(Luke 4:22)

Among
the townspeople with
whom He was familiar, He
was known as **Joseph's Son**, the
carpenter of Nazareth. We know
Him instead as a skilled craftsman
Who possessed the vision and
the power to transform raw
materials into objects
of transcendent
beauty.

October 28

The
Light of Life
(John 8:12)

Those
who work in
secret, their motivation
pure and without guile, are
as children of **The Light of
Life**, who joyously give
Him all of the
credit.

October 29

The Messiah
(Daniel 9:25)

There
are special
moments when our
rapport with **The Messiah** is
so personal and is so profoundly
moving that it is meaningful only to
ourselves. Because our feelings testify so
sweetly of His love, care, and concern,
and because sacred principles are so
often sensed more easily than they
are expressed, they cannot be
shared with others whose
frame of reference may
be more profane.

October 30

My Beloved and Chosen from the Beginning
(Moses 4:2)

The
**Beloved
and Chosen
from the Beginning**
has set the example, that
all might follow Him. Even now,
His disciples can hear a reverberating
echo of the approving declaration
uttered so long ago: "This is my
beloved Son, in whom I
am well pleased."
(Matthew 3:17).

October 31

The Son of
the Most High God
(Mark 5:7)

The unity
of the Godhead is
illustrated by completeness.
The Son of the Most High God is
one with the Father and the Holy Ghost,
seeing, as each of Them does, with the
eye of perfection. They understand
alike, and are guided by the
same unerring principle
of equity.

November 1

The
Son of Man
(Matthew 16:27)

**The
Son of Man**
of Holiness revealed a
great truth about the Divine
Nature, when He said: "No man
knoweth the Son, but the Father,
neither knoweth any man the
Father, save the Son."
(Matthew 11:27).

November 2

The Resurrection and the Life
(John 11:25)

Have greater words than these ever been spoken since the foundation of the world? "I am **The Resurrection and the Life**: he that believeth in me, though he were dead, yet shall he live." (John 11:25).

November 3

I Am
that I Am
(Exodus 3:14)

Somewhere within
the incomprehensible expanse
of the infinite and eternal universe,
and before the Wise Men of the East gazed
skyward, before the rise of civilization, before
life had burst forth in profousion on the earth,
before the continents took their present form,
when there were neither seasons nor days,
nor beginning nor end of years, and
when time itself did not yet exist,
was **I Am that I Am**.

November 4

Our Master
(Matthew 23:8)

The
evidence of faith
is the receipt of signs
that we receive only after we
accept the truth. These miracles
can be ours as long as we
allow the Lord to be
Our Master.

November 5

Omega
(Revelation 1:11)

At
the end of time,
when the earth has had
its final curtain call, the sun has
exhausted its remaining fuel, and the
universe itself has stopped expanding,
Omega, the Last, will still bear rule over
all of His creations. He will maintain
order and balance in the cosmos,
and all that lies therein will
forever remain within
His dominion.

November 6

The Carpenter's Son
(Matthew 13:55)

We don't see things as they are. Instead, we see things as we are. Some only see **The Carpenter's Son**, while others immediately drop to their knees in adoration of the Savior of the world.

November 7

The
Father of Spirits
(Hebrews 12:9)

At the
conclusion of
our mission farewell
in the pre-earth existence, the
veil was drawn across our eyes and
our minds. It was in such a distant realm
that it remains hidden from our view. Only
in shadows of memory and inarticulate
impressions do we sense **The Father
of Spirits** Who has never stopped
guiding us with parental
encouragement.

November 8

The
King of Heaven
(2 Nephi 10:14)

In all
the mansions of
our Heavenly Father,
in the realm of glory that is
a celebration of dazzling light
and piercing truth, where pure
intelligence freely flows, and the
souls of the Just are quickened by
an inexhaustible supply of celestial
energy, there is One Who is greater
than all, in might, majesty, power
and dominion: He to Whom
we pay homage as **The
King of Heaven**.

November 9

The Mighty One of Israel
(1 Nephi 22:12)

The Mighty One of Israel has promised us that we shall find rest in Zion, a city and state of mind that practices repentance in both its form and in its substance. With a solid grasp on that which is real, she knows how to deal in spiritual absolutes, and is grounded on the bedrock of principle.

November 10

The Lord is my Helper
(Hebrews 13:6)

Life sometimes administers the test before we've had a chance to study the lesson. Experience can be one of our most demanding teachers. **The Lord is my Helper** and He stands ready to minister to me, should I earn less than an A+ grade on any pop quiz.

November 11

A Propitiation through Faith
(Romans 3:25)

One of the temptations of life is to confuse dreams with reality, but if our dreams are surrendered to a narrow reality that is defined by sensuality and worldliness, we will surely suffer a spiritual defeat of cosmic proportion. When we trust in the Lord, however, we ground ourselves on the solid bedrock of eternal truth. He becomes **A Propitiation through Faith**.

November 12

The Redeemer of Israel
(John 11:25)

Our Lord and Savior Jesus Christ is a resurrected Man of Holiness and **The Redeemer of Israel**. He does not selfishly guard His perfection, but instead glories in the possibility that those who obey Him and endure to the end may become like Him, even flawless. We strive to conform our lives to images that have been captured with a celestial lens, of Him and His Father in Heaven Who are perfect.

November 13

(Him Who) Bare our Sins in His Own Body
(1 Peter 2:24)

As our comprehension expands, so does our responsibility and commitment to obedience. When our lives are in harmony with Gospel principles, we are in a constant state of improvement that will ultimately lead to perfection. We cannot be saved in ignorance of that knowledge. Work we must, but lunch is free, provided by Him Who **Bare our Sins in His Own Body**.

November 14

He is my Rock and my Salvation
(Psalms 62:2)

I must not describe the Lord in comfortably contemporary terms that are less reflections of His divine nature, and more the expressions of my own insecurities. His Spirit provides the definition of His character. It tells me that **He is my Rock and my Salvation**, the same yesterday, today, and forever, and that He can be known.

November 15

The Father and the Son
(2 John 1:9)

Mashed potatoes and
gravy, or apple pie and ice cream.
Love and marriage, or a horse and carriage.
Night and day, or thunder and lightning.
Sugar and spice, and everything nice.
Roses are red, violets are blue. **The
Father and the Son** are the names
that are inseparably uttered by
the faithful in one and
the same breath.

November 16

The
Light
(John 1:7-8)

As we journey
through mortality,
celestial sign posts have
been provided as our guides
by **The Light** that never faileth.
He is an attentive chaperone Who
illuminates a path of safety so that
we might avoid telestial traffic circles
and conceptual cul-de-sacs that would
take us on detours away from the
strait and narrow way.

November 17

The Lawgiver, Who is Able to Save
(James 4:12)

We believe that the Lord is a **Lawgiver, Who is Able to Save**; that Jesus can be our Sure Companion; that His Rest is nothing less than exaltation in the mansions of the Celestial Kingdom of God

November 18

(He Is Ready to) Judge the Quick and the Dead
(2 Timothy 4:1)

He is
Ready to **Judge
the Quick and the Dead**
and there will come a time when
we realize there is nowhere we can hide;
when we are faced with the stark realization
that we can no longer take pleasure in
iniquity. As Alma counseled his
son Corianton: "Wickedness
never was happiness."
(Alma 41:10)

November 19

The Living and True God
(1 Thessalonians 1:9)

We
live in a tight
knit community of
true believers that has
the reassurance to know
that **The Living and True God** stands at
the head of His
Church.

November 20

The
Just One
(Acts 7:52)

He is
just one, but
to me He matters
most, and He is still
more than all the rest
combined. In Him, we
live and move and have
our being. He is just one,
about Whom we preach,
teach, expound, exhort,
and prophesy. But He
is more than just one.
He is **The Just
One.**

November 21

The Light and the Redeemer of the World
(Doctrine & Covenants 93:9)

We
believe that
He is **The Light and
the Redeemer of the World**.
We believe that being a Christian
is less about fitting into a mold, and
more about having a personal
relationship with God that
is consistent with the
revelation of His
Son.

November 22

Peniel
(Genesis 32:30)

If you have held a
newborn in your arms,
or stared death in the face;
or if you have stood on the top
of a mountain, or knelt quietly in
a sacred grove, or if you have lingered
reverently in the Lord's temple, or have
held the hand of a trusting child, you
have seen **Peniel**, even the very
face of God, and you
have lived!

November 23

The Lord of the Sabbath
(Mark 2:28)

It used to
be called the Holy
Sabbath. Later, just the
Sabbath. Until recently, Sunday.
Now, it's the weekend; a time when
wander and play have replaced ponder
and pray. In spite of all of our religious
restructuring, rationalization, self-
denial, and indifference, He
remains **The Lord of
the Sabbath**.

November 24

(He Who was made) Lower than the Angels for the Suffering of Death
(Hebrews 2:9)

We
are only
recently removed
from the presence of God,
where none may come to hurt or
make afraid, into a world of challenging
trials and daunting adversity. In short, we are
spiritual beings now having mortal experiences.
But He was unique. He came from the throne
of heaven with His eyes wide open and He
was subsequently made **Lower than the
Angels for the Suffering of Death**,
and still, He prevailed over all.

November 25

The Lord both of the Dead and Living
(Romans 14:9)

When we pass from mortality into the world of Spirits, and the veil of forgetfulness is lifted from our eyes and our minds, we will recognize with stunning sobriety our Master, **The Lord both of the Dead and Living,** Who will reach out and quicken our memory of the promises we have made and the covenants we have kept.

November 26

The
Chief Cornerstone
(Ephesians 2:20)

We try, but
our puny efforts seem
to be so inadequate. We patch
together a semblance of order, but
sometimes deceive ourselves with the
creations of our own making. While
ever so quietly in the background,
the peaceful voice of conscience
gently reminds us just Who is
The Chief Cornerstone
of our existence.

November 27

A New
and Living Way
(Hebrews 10:20)

He Who hath
consecrated **A New
and Living Way** asks us
to carry our burdens just a
little longer and further. He
knows that when we are urged
to go the second mile, we are being
given an invitation to become spiritually
independent, as we are awakened to a
greater appreciation of the tangible
and intangible rewards for our
sustained efforts.

November 28

Our Father, our Redeemer
(Isaiah 63:16)

There is no warmth in clothes that are not worn, strength in food that is not eaten, or power in faith that does not embrace works. In the end, even though we rely on the merits of **Our Father, our Redeemer**, and are saved by His grace, work we must, to merit our salvation.

November 29

A Great God and a Great King
(Psalms 95:3)

**A
Great God
and a Great King**
has promised the Saints
that they shall safely dwell
in Zion, a city that stands
as a stellar example that
the reward of faith
is celestial
surety.

November 30

(He Who was) Consecrated for Evermore
(Hebrews 7:28)

He Who was
Consecrated for Evermore
has given us laws that demand
that we give heed to the way we spend
our time, and also to the care with which
we make time, the diligence with which we
find time, and the discipline we exhibit in
taking time. The laws of the Celestial
Kingdom allow us to create more
time, but forbid us to waste it,
or to kill time.

December 1

Jesus of Nazareth
(Matthew 26:71)

Before we received **Jesus of Nazareth** in our hearts, we stood on neutral ground. Since we made the covenant of baptism, however, we can be hot or we can be cold, but we can never again have it both ways.

December 2

The Propitiation for our Sins
(1 John 4:10)

The Pharisees criticized Him when He mingled with the wrong crowd consisting of publicans and sinners. Did they not realize that they who were whole were not the ones who needed a physician, but them that were sick? He came to save us from our telestial tendencies, and is **The Propitiation for our Sins**.

December 3

One God and Father of All
(Ephesians 4:6)

Each
one of us
will some day
have a chance to
tell our own personal
story to the **One God and
Father of All**. We will need to
be candid and forthright, for our
record will have been written "not
with ink, but with the Spirit of
the living God. Not in tables
of stone, but in (the) fleshy
tables of the heart."
(2 Corinthians 3:3).

December 4

Christ
(1 John 5:1)

Every
discussion of faith must
distinguish it from its caricatures.
In its initial stages, it is not knowledge.
It is not just wishful thinking, nor is it naiveté.
It is not a reality check for the hopelessly romantic.
It is not a remedy for those whose lamps are
without oil. It is not overdraft protection
for our spiritual bank accounts. Faith
inspires us with confidence that life
is a school of discipline whose
Author and Teacher
is **Christ**.

December 5

The Heir
of all Things
(Hebrews 1:2)

It is
sometimes
called free agency.
But we know that it is
really quite expensive. Some
use it to barter for telestial toys,
and to live only for the moment,
while others remember that they
have been given an endowment
from **The Heir of all Things**,
that they might wisely use
their agency to thereby
safeguard celestial
sureties.

December 6

The Chief Shepherd
(1 Peter 5:4)

The true doctrine of **The Chief Shepherd** is our defense and our fortification, and obedience to the covenants can be our sanctuary from the ravenous wolves and winds of wickedness that continually harass the flock.

December 7

The
King of Saints
(Revelation 15:3)

Our
acknowledgment of the
Lord Jesus Christ as **The King of
Saints** trains our thoughts on those
experiences that repetitively reinforce
the shadow of another time and space;
those things that are reflected by
Gospel ordinances that cannot
be revealed to the world,
for they are symbolic,
and can only be
discerned by
the Spirit.

December 8

He that Liveth and was Dead
(Revelation 1:18)

How can we hope to comprehend God, or **He that Liveth and was Dead**? Clearly, we are dealing with two orders of mind. "For my thoughts are not your thoughts, neither are your ways my ways, saith the Lord. For as the heavens are higher than the earth, so are my thoughts than your thoughts." (Isaiah 55:8).

December 9

A
Great Light
(Matthew 4:16)

The simple
acknowledgment of our
Lord and Savior Jesus Christ
as **A Great Light** establishes a new
faculty of knowledge, by which we receive
understanding that could not have been obtained
were our spirits to have remained imprisoned within
our bodies. Our greater comprehension provides a fresh
perspective, expands our powers of observation, and
liberates our minds to embrace the Holy Ghost, as
we freely wander among eternal principles, and
with stunning clarity focus our attention
on spiritual truth.

December 10

The Light
of the World
(John 8:12)

Long ago,
Wise Men traveled
from the East, following a
Star that would lead them to
a manger in Bethlehem. Those
who seek Him today are guided
by the very same **Light of
the World** directly to
its Source.

December 11

The Fountain
of the Water of Life
(Revelation 21:6)

We are
never sure that the
water we drink is free
from harmful contaminants.
But we are certain of the purity
of the soul-sustaining spiritual
sustenance of **The Fountain of
the Water of Life**, the very
element introduced so
long ago to the
woman at the
well.

December 12

The Lord is a God of Knowledge
(1 Samuel 2:3)

The Lord is a God of Knowledge and is mighty in faith. These are the joint powers by which worlds were created and by which, out of chaos, order was brought to the heavens. By these eternal forces, the land, sea, and sky recognize His voice and obey His will. There is nothing He does not know, nothing He cannot do, and His eye pierces all things, else He would cease to be God.

December 13

The Lord God of our Fathers
(Deuteronomy 26:7)

In the
Last Days, we
ask who will accept
the son of the carpenter as
The Lord God of our Fathers?
The same people who would have
prostrated themselves before
Him and worshipped Him
as the promised Messiah
had they lived in
His day.

December 14

Christ,
Who is our Life
(Colossians 3:4)

The Holy
Babe of Bethlehem,
Christ, Who is our Life,
was cradled in His mother's
arms, surrounded by the pungent
aroma of sheep and straw. Among the
heavenly host, angels celebrated His birth,
while all the sons and daughters of God
shouted for joy, shepherds knelt beside
the manger, and wise men obediently
followed His star from the East.

December 15

God Who Quickeneth all Things
(1 Timothy 6:13)

As He endured
unimaginable suffering in the Garden
of Gethsemane, it is ironic that it was Jesus Christ,
the **God Who Quickeneth all Things** and in Whom
resided the power to give life to all of creation, Who
Himself needed the sustaining influence that was
provided by His Father's angels throughout
that excruciating torment. But as a result
of His determination, faith, knowledge,
and power, in the end, the influence
of His sacrifice would extend all
the way to the furthest reaches
of eternity, somehow making
possible an Infinite
Atonement.

December 16

(He) is Faithful and Just
(1 John 1:9)

He Who is
Faithful and Just
taught that our righteous application of moral agency is irrevocably related to the acquisition of knowledge. Those with greater awareness are responsible to live in accordance with the light they have received. In contrast to those who may have ignorantly sinned, they bear the greater condemnation should they turn against the truth.

December 17

God
is Faithful
(1 Corinthians 10:13)

God is Faithful, and by giving
Him our unqualified devotion, we can
achieve the highest pinnacle of spiritual life.
Not the false security that is the begrudging result
of misguided trust, but the assurance that comes
from yielding our will to His, that springs from
our knowledge of His unwavering fidelity,
and that flows from our unshakable
confidence in His love for us.

December 18

The Head
of the Body
(Colossians 1:18)

Our feet can take us down crooked paths.
Our hands can lead us into temptation.
Our tongues can speak lies and deceit.
Our hearts can move us to passion.
Our voices can be raised in anger.
But we pass through all of these
telestial trials and move on
to celestial sureties by
**The Head of the
Body**.

December 19

**The Christ, the
Son of the Living God**
(Matthew 16:16)

He is
**The Christ, the
Son of the Living God.**
All the earth, and everything
thereon, is His footstool. We leave
to His better judgment the bestowal
of its treasures, and turn our attention
instead, to the more valuable
riches of eternity.

December 20

The Most High
over all the Earth
(Psalms 83:18)

It is
**The Most High
over all the Earth** Who
maintains order among His
vast creations. At His command,
the elements instantly obey. In the
clarifying luminosity of all eternity,
His eye pierces both the beginning
and the end, and all that lies in
between, and there is nothing
that can escape His
attention.

December 21

God
the Father
(1 Peter 1:2)

He sent
His Son into the
world to do a work no
other could perform. **God
the Father**, Who was the wisest
of all, bestowed upon mankind His
matchless Gift, and set in motion
forces that would culminate in
the power to transcend
time and space.

December 22

A Personage Whose Brightness and Glory Defy all Description
(Joseph Smith History 1:17)

Long before
the shining new star
appeared in the night sky
above Bethlehem, and before
the prophets foretold His birth,
He lived as **A Personage Whose
Brightness and Glory Defy
all Description.**

December 23

The
Son of Mary
(Mark 6:3)

How utterly profound
must have been her astonishment,
to have both angels and the heavenly
host attend to her, to receive shepherds
who sought her babe in the stable, and to
entertain Wise Men who had traveled
from the East with offerings of gold,
and frankincense, and myrrh. All
for the sake of the Holy Child,
The Son of Mary.

December 24

The Express Image
of God's Person
(Hebrews 1:3)

"I bring
good tidings of
great joy." (Luke 2:10).
The angel's announcement had
an ancestral ring, and struck familiar
chords of memory. It heralded the
bestowal of the most intimate of
gifts, even the Savior of the
world, **The Express Image
of God's Person**, His
Son Jesus.

December 25

Holy Child
(Moroni 8:3)

Saints and sinners worship on Christmas Day.
Faith is wrought on earth on Christmas Day.
Eyes of children sparkle on Christmas Day.
Mankind is reconciled on Christmas Day.
Peace reigns supreme on Christmas Day.
Charity never faileth on Christmas Day.
Music fills the air on Christmas Day.
The **Holy Child** Jesus is born
on Christmas Day.

December 26

The Seed
of the Woman
(Genesis 3:15)

Her holy mission
was to join with God in the
mystery and wonder of creation.
With the elements of blood and water,
she brought new life into the world. **The
Seed of the Woman** was of lowly birth,
inasmuch as He was brought forth
in a manger. But the angels who
attended Him that night
called Him the Son of
the Highest.

December 27

God's Holy Child Jesus
(Acts 4:27)

**God's
Holy Child Jesus**
came from His presence
just as every newborn has
since the beginning of time. "Our
birth is but a sleep and a forgetting. The
soul that rises with us, our life's star, hath
had elsewhere it's setting, and cometh from
afar. Not in entire forgetfulness, and not in
utter nakedness, but trailing clouds of
glory do we come, from God,
Who is our Home."
(Wordsworth).

December 28

King
of the Jews
(Matthew 2:2)

Wise men who had followed the bright and shining star from a far country boldly inquired of Herod: "Where is he that is born **King of the Jews**?" (Matthew 2:1-2). Their Christmas message was confirmation that the notable, the foreign born, and the wealthy, may also come unto Christ.

December 29

The Firstfruits of Them that Slept
(1 Corinthians 15:20)

The
empty tomb in
a quiet garden outside
the city walls is even today
peacefully still, bearing silent
witness to the resurrection's reality.
The Firstfruits of Them that Slept
ushered in a renewal that none
who had ever lived on the
earth had known.

December 30

The King that Cometh in the Name of the Lord
(Luke 19:38)

All of the prophets since the world began have testified of **The King that Cometh in the Name of the Lord**, and many signs and wonders have been given. Types and shadows have been raised up for the benefit of all those who have eyes to see and ears to hear.

December 31

Him which is Perfect in Knowledge
(Job 37:16)

Faith,
together with
the comprehension of
eternal principles existing in
unqualified harmony with each
other, typifies the very pinnacle of
organized existence and the rule
of Heaven observed by **Him
which is Perfect in
Knowledge**.

The End

Minute Musings

Spontaneous Combustions of Thought

Volume One

Appendix One

A Chronological List of
366 Scriptural References to Jesus Christ

"That which cometh from above is sacred, and must be
spoken with care, and by constraint of the Spirit."
(Doctrine & Covenants 63:64).

compiled by

Philip M. Hudson

January

1. Wonderful (Isaiah 9:6)
2. The Judge of all the Earth (Genesis 18:25)
3. Righteous Man (Luke 23:47)
4. The Fear of God (Genesis 20:11)
5. He that Hath the Key of David (Revelation 3:7)
6. Everlasting God, the Lord, the Creator of the Ends of the Earth (Isaiah 40:28)
7. The Mighty One of Jacob (Isaiah 60:16)
8. He who Gave Himself for our Sins (Galatians 1:4)
9. The Word of Life (1 John 1:1)
10. The Lord He is God (Deuteronomy 4:35)
11. He Who is Able to Save to the Uttermost (Hebrews 7:25)
12. Lord from Heaven (1 Corinthians 15:47)
13. The Prophet of Nazareth (Matthew 21:11)
14. He Who was Prepared From the Foundation of the World (Ether 3:14)
15. Counsellor (Isaiah 9:6)
16. Rabbi (John 1:38)
17. The Carpenter (Mark 6:3)
18. The Bread of Life (John 6:35)
19. The Great King (Malachi 1:14)
20. The Lord the Righteous Judge (2 Timothy 4:8)
21. The Word (John 1:1)
22. The Lord our God is One Lord (Deuteronomy 6:4)
23. A Brazen Serpent (Helaman 8:14)
24. The Strength of the Children of Israel (Joel 3:16)
25. Him who Suffered Without the Gate (Hebrews 13:12)
26. The Father of Lights (James 1:17)
27. Amen (John 14:6)
28. Excellent is Thy Name (Psalms 8:1)
29. The Prince of Life (Acts 3:15)
30. A Nazarene (Matthew 2:23)
31. The First and the Last (Isaiah 44:6)

February

1. Wisdom, Righteousness, Sanctification, and Redemption unto Us (1 Corinthians 1:30)
2. The God of my Salvation (Psalms 18:46)
3. The Sun of Righteousness (Malachi 4:2)
4. The Creator of the Ends of the Earth (Isaiah 40:28)
5. The Brightness of God's Glory (Hebrews 1:3)
6. The Lord God of the Holy Prophets (Revelation 22:6)
7. The Lord is our Judge; the Lord is our Lawgiver (Isaiah 33:22)
8. The Root and the Offspring of David (Revelation 22:16)
9. Holy, Holy, Holy (Isaiah 6:3)
10. Jesus Christ of Nazareth (Acts 4:10)
11. He Who is Passed into the Heavens (Hebrews 4:14)
12. Him Who Healeth the People (2 Chronicles 3:20)
13. A Minister of the Circumcision for the Truth of God (Romans 15:8)
14. Abba, Father (Mark 14:36)
15. God, the Greatest of All (Doctrine & Covenants 19:18)
16. The Lord that Healeth (Exodus 15:26)
17. A Living Stone (1 Peter 2:4)
18. A Righteous Judge (2 Timothy 4:8)
19. The First Begotten (Hebrews 1:6)
20. He Who Tasted Death for Every Man (Hebrews 2:9)
21. He who is Counted Worthy of More Glory Than Moses (Hebrews 3:3)
22. The Hope of Israel (Acts 28:20)
23. The Beginning and the End (Revelation 22:13)
24. The Lord God of Hosts (Isaiah 10:24)
25. The Head of Every Man (1 Corinthians 11:3)
26. He who Uphold(s) All Things by the Word of His Power (Hebrews 1:3)
27. An Example (John 13:15)
28. The God of Beth-el (Genesis 31:13)
29. The King, Whose name is the Lord of Hosts (Jeremiah 46:18)

March

1 He who is Able to Succor Them that are Tempted (Hebrews 2:18)
2 The Beloved Son of God (Matthew 3:17)
3 Him who Learned Obedience by the Things which He Suffered (Hebrews 5:8)
4 The Lord Jesus (Luke 24:3)
5 He Who Gave Himself for Us (Titus 2:14)
6 The Only Begotten Son (John 1:14)
7 The King Eternal (1 Timothy 1:17)
8 (He Who is) Without Sin unto Salvation (Hebrews 9:28)
9 The Only Wise God our Savior (Jude 1:25)
10 The Consolation of Israel (Luke 2:25)
11 God the Judge of All (Hebrews 12:23)
12 The Son of David (Matthew 12:23)
13 The Light of Men (John 1:4)
14 A True Light, which Lighteth every Man (John 1:9)
15 Living Water (John 4:10)
16 The Lord of Glory (James 2:1)
17 A Surety of a Better Testament (Hebrews 7:22)
18 He Who Came into the World to Save Sinners (1 Timothy 1:15)
19 Christ, the Chosen of God (Luke 23:35)
20 The Bridegroom (Matthew 9:15)
21 Jesus the Son of God (Hebrews 4:14)
22 The Strength of Israel (1 Samuel 15:29)
23 The Savior Jesus Christ (Mormon 3:14)
24 The God of Israel (2 Nephi 25:14)
25 God's Anointed (Acts 4:27)
26 The King (Isaiah 6:5)
27 Chosen of God (John 23:35)
28 The Father of Heaven and of Earth (2 Nephi 25:12)
29 A Merciful and Faithful High Priest (Hebrews 2:17)
30 The Great Jehovah (Doctrine & Covenants 128:9)
31 A True Vine (John 15:1)

April

1. He Who Sitteth on the Right Hand of God (Colossians 3:1)
2. The High and Lofty One that Inhabits Eternity (Isaiah 57:15)
3. He Who was Raised from the Dead (2 Timothy 2:8)
4. The Creator of Israel (Isaiah 43:15)
5. The Lord the God of Heaven (Jonah 1:9)
6. A Bright and Morning Star (Revelation 22:16)
7. Jehovah, the Eternal Judge (Moroni 10:34)
8. The Son of God (Romans 1:4)
9. He Who Died and Rose Again (1 Thessalonians 4:14)
10. Jesus Christ the Righteous (1 John 2:1)
11. The Savior of the World (John 4:42)
12. The Zeal of the Lord of Hosts (2 Kings 19:31)
13. The Word of God (Revelation 19:13)
14. A Great God (Titus 2:13)
15. The Anointed One (Psalms 2:2)
16. The Author and Finisher of our Faith (Hebrews 12:2)
17. The Mighty God (Isaiah 9:6)
18. The Image of God (2 Corinthians 4:4)
19. Jesus of Galilee (Matthew 26:29)
20. The Judge of Quick and Dead (Acts 10:42)
21. A Serpent of Brass (Alma 33:19)
22. He is Good (Psalms 34:8)
23. A Righteous Branch (Jeremiah 23:5)
24. Apostle (Hebrews 3:1-2)
25. God is Love (1 John 4:8)
26. The Lamb Slain from before the Foundation of the World (Revelation 13:8)
27. The Light, and the Life, and the Truth (Ether 4:12)
28. The Lord of Heaven and Earth (Matthew 11:25)
29. The Lord God Almighty (2 Nephi 28:15)
30. The Living God (Joshua 3:10)

May

1 Our Advocate with the Father (1 John 2:1)
2 The Creator (1 Peter 4:19)
3 The Lord your God is God of Gods (Deuteronomy 10:17)
4 The Firstborn (Romans 8:29)
5 Living Father (John 6:57)
6 Rabboni (John 20:16)
7 The Rock (1 Samuel 2:2)
8 The Son of the Eternal Father (1 Nephi 13:40)
9 He Who Did no Sin (1 Peter 2:22)
10 Jesus Christ His Son (1 John 1:7)
11 Faithful and True (Revelation 19:11)
12 The Head of the Church (Ephesians 5:23)
13 The Good Shepherd (John 10:14)
14 That Great Shepherd of the Sheep (Hebrews 13:20)
15 He Who Came by Water and Blood (1 John 5:6)
16 A High Priest after the Order of Melchizedek (Hebrews 5:10)
17 I Am the Law, and the Light (3 Nephi 15:9)
18 Jesus (Romans 3:26)
19 Lord God of the Hebrews (Exodus 7:16)
20 God (Malachi 1:11)
21 A Shadow of Heavenly Things (Hebrews 8:5)
22 He Who put away Sin by the Sacrifice of Himself (Hebrews 9:26)
23 The Rock of His Salvation (Deuteronomy 32:15)
24 The Savior (Matthew 1:21)
25 Shepherd of Israel (Psalms 80:1)
26 The God of thy Father (Genesis 46:3)
27 The God of Abraham, the God of Isaac, the God of Jacob (Exodus 3:6)
28 A Faithful Witness (Revelation 1:5)
29 A Fellowservant (Revelation 22:9)
30 The Glory of the God of Israel (Ezekiel 9:3)
31 God and His Father (Revelation 1:6)

June

1. God and the Father (James 1:27)
2. The God of the Whole Earth (Isaiah 54:5)
3. The Lord of Lords (1 Timothy 6:15)
4. Christ the Lamb (Doctrine & Covenants 76:85)
5. The Savior of the Body (Ephesians 5:23)
6. Him Which is, and Which Was, and Which is to Come (Revelation 1:8)
7. A Spiritual Rock (1 Corinthians 10:4)
8. The Spirit of Truth (John 14:17)
9. The Son Jesus Christ our Lord (1 John 5:20)
10. The Example of the Son (2 Nephi 31:16)
11. Counselor (2 Nephi 18:6)
12. Jesus Christ (Ephesians 2:20)
13. Him in Whom is Eternal Life (1 John 5:11)
14. The Lord of the Whole Earth (Doctrine & Covenants 55:1)
15. Lord God Omnipotent (Mosiah 3:21)
16. The Son of the Living God (Matthew 16:16)
17. The End of the Law for Righteousness (Romans 10:4)
18. A Shadow of Things to Come (Colossians 2:17)
19. The Prophet of the Highest (Luke 1:76)
20. The Holy One of Israel (Psalms 89:18)
21. The Lamb that was Slain (Revelation 5:12)
22. Father (Acts 1:4)
23. The Root of David (Revelation 5:5)
24. The Lord of the Vineyard (Jacob 5:75)
25. The Redeemer of the World (Doctrine & Covenants 93:9)
26. Their Great and True Shepherd (Helaman 15:13)
27. God our Savior (Jude 1:25)
28. He Who by Himself Purged our Sins (Hebrews 1:3)
29. The Mediator (1 Timothy 2:5)
30. The Rock of Heaven (Moses 7:53)

July

1. Offered Himself without Spot (Hebrews 9:11)
2. A Priest Forever after the Order of Melchizedek (Psalms 110:4)
3. A Fountain of Living Waters (Jeremiah 2:13)
4. One Having Authority (Matthew 7:29)
5. God of my Rock, my Shield, and the Horn of my Salvation, my High Tower, and my Refuge, my Savior (2 Samuel 22:3)
6. Holy, Harmless [and] Undefiled (Hebrews 7:26)
7. Our Lord and Saviour (2 Peter 3:2)
8. The Lamb (Revelation 5:5)
9. The Most High God (3 Nephi 11:17)
10. The Lord God of Abraham (Genesis 28:13)
11. The Seed of Abraham (Galatians 3:16)
12. Messias (John 4:25)
13. The Stone of Israel (Doctrine & Covenants 50:44)
14. The Way, the Truth, and the Life (John 14:6)
15. He Who Knew no Sin (2 Corinthians 5:21)
16. The Lord is the Strength of my Life (Psalms 27:1)
17. Lord Our Righteousness (Jeremiah 23:6)
18. He who is Made Higher than the Heavens (Hebrews 7:26)
19. Emmanuel (Matthew 1:23)
20. The Foundation of the Church (1 Corinthians 3:11)
21. God our Father and the Lord Jesus Christ (Romans 1:7)
22. Him in Whom is Salvation (2 Timothy 2:10)
23. Him Who Hath Perfected Forever them that are Sanctified (Hebrews 10:14)
24. The Lord Even of the Sabbath (Matthew 12:8)
25. A Branch (Isaiah 11:1)
26. The Savior of Israel (Acts 13:23)
27. The Governor that Shall Rule Israel (Matthew 2:6)
28. Alpha and Omega (Revelation 1:11)
29. The Bishop of your Souls (2 Peter 2:25)
30. The King of all the Earth (Psalms 47:7)
31. A Lamb Without Blemish and Without Spot (1 Peter 1:19)

August

1. The Living God and an Everlasting King (Jeremiah 10:10)
2. A Stone (Jacob 4:15)
3. Judge of Both the Quick and the Dead (Acts 10:42)
4. Light of Israel (2 Nephi 20:17)
5. Son of the Highest (Luke 1:32)
6. Our Passover (Hebrews 13:1)
7. The Mighty God of Jacob (Psalms 132:2)
8. The Mediator of a Better Covenant (Hebrews 8:6)
9. The Almighty (Revelation 1:8)
10. He who is Better than the Angels (Hebrews 1:4)
11. There is One God, and One Mediator Between God and Man, the Man Christ Jesus (1 Timothy 2:51)
12. The Lord God (Jude 1:4)
13. The Forerunner (Hebrews 6:20)
14. The Living Bread Which Came Down from Heaven (John 6:51)
15. The Witness of God (1 John 5:9)
16. A Teacher Come From God (John 3:2)
17. He who Made Angels, Authorities, and Powers…Subject to Him (1 Peter 3:22)
18. Holy One, the Creator of Israel (Isaiah 43:15)
19. God and Father of our Lord Jesus Christ (1 Peter 1:3)
20. He who Hath Given us Understanding that we may know Him that is True (1 John 5:20)
21. The Almighty God (Genesis 17:1)
22. The Great Creator (Jacob 3:7)
23. The Lord Jehovah (Isaiah 12:2)
24. The Lord the King of Israel (Isaiah 44:6)
25. The God of the Hebrews (Exodus 5:3)
26. The Seed of David (2 Timothy 2:8)
27. The Author of Eternal Salvation (Hebrews 5:9)
28. The Lord, for He is our God (Joshua 24:18)
29. A Refiner's Fire (Malachi 3:2)
30. The Lord God of your Fathers (Deuteronomy 1:11)
31. The Mediator of the New Testament (Hebrews 9:15)

September

1 Christ Jesus (Romans 3:24)
2 Our Captain (2 Chronicles 13:12)
3 He who is Crowned with Glory and Honour (Hebrews 2:9)
4 He Who Hath Obtained Eternal Redemption for Us (Hebrews 9:12)
5 The Blessed of God (Psalms 45:2)
6 The Minister of the Sanctuary and of the True Tabernacle (Hebrews 8:2)
7 Our Lawgiver (Isaiah 33:22)
8 Our Heavenly King (Mosiah 2:19)
9 The Prince of the Kings of the Earth (Revelation 1:5)
10 He in Whom are Hid all the Treasures of Wisdom and Knowledge (Colossians 2:3)
11 The High Calling of God (Philippians 3:14)
12 I Am (John 8:58)
13 One with the Father (John 10:30)
14 Their Rock and their Salvation (1 Nephi 15:15)
15 He who Hath an Unchangeable Priesthood (Hebrews 7:24)
16 An Offering and Sacrifice to God (Ephesians 5:2)
17 Maker (Hosea 8:14)
18 Merciful (2 Chronicles 30:9)
19 The Lord of Hosts (Isaiah 5:16)
20 Our Deliverer (Romans 11:16)
21 The Apostle and High Priest of our Profession (Hebrews 3:1)
22 A Light to Lighten the Gentiles (Luke 2:32)
23 Our Redeemer (Isaiah 59:20)
24 The Propitiation for the Sins of the Whole World (1 John 2:2)
25 The Son of the Blessed (Mark 14:61)
26 The God over all the Earth (1 Nephi 11:6)
27 Our Shield (Genesis 15:1)
28 The Holiest of All (Hebrews 9:3)
29 The Creator of Heaven and Earth (Jacob 2:5)
30 The Rock of my Strength (Isaiah 17:10)

October

1 Blessed for Evermore (2 Corinthians 11:31)
2 A High Priest of Good Things to Come (Hebrews 9:11)
3 Christ of God (John 9:20)
4 Jehovah, Mighty God of Jacob (Doctrine & Covenants 109:68)
5 The Lord of All (Acts 10:36)
6 The Highest of All (Doctrine & Covenants 76:70)
7 Jesus Christ the Son of God, the Father of Heaven and Earth, the Creator of all Things from the Beginning (Mosiah 3:8)
8 The Hope of His People (Joel 3:16)
9 The Horn of David (Psalms 132:17)
10 The Messenger of the Covenant (Malachi 3:1)
11 One Eternal God (Alma 11:44)
12 Shiloh (Ezekiel 21:27)
13 Lord (Matthew 28:6)
14 The Prince of Peace (Isaiah 9:6)
15 The Head Stone of the Corner (Psalms 118:22)
16 The Very Eternal Father of Heaven and of Earth (Alma 11:39)
17 Jehovah (Exodus 6:3)
18 An Everlasting Light (Isaiah 60:19)
19 I am the Law and the Light (3 Nephi 15:9)
20 Holy One and the Just (Acts 3:14)
21 The Door of the Sheep (John 10:7)
22 The First Begotten of the Dead (Revelation 1:5)
23 The Law, and the Life, and the Truth (Ether 4:12)
24 The Captain of our Salvation (Hebrews 2:10)
25 Author (Moroni 6:4)
26 He Who was Sent that we Might Live Through Him (1 John 4:9)
27 Joseph's Son (Luke 4:22)
28 The Light of Life (John 8:12)
29 The Messiah (Daniel 9:25)
30 My Beloved and Chosen from the Beginning (Moses 4:2)
31 The Son of the Most High God (Mark 5:7)

November

1. The Son of Man (Matthew 16:27)
2. The Resurrection and the Life (John 11:25)
3. I Am that I Am (Exodus 3:14)
4. Master (Matthew 23:8)
5. Omega (Revelation 1:11)
6. The Carpenter's Son (Matthew 13:55)
7. The Father of Spirits (Hebrews 12:9)
8. The King of Heaven (2 Nephi 10:14)
9. The Mighty One of Israel (1 Nephi 22:12)
10. The Lord is my Helper (Hebrews 13:6)
11. A Propitiation through Faith (Romans 3:25)
12. The Redeemer of Israel (John 11:25)
13. He Who Bare our Sins in His Own Body (1 Peter 2:24)
14. He is my Rock and my Salvation (Psalms 62:2)
15. The Father and the Son (2 John 1:9)
16. The Light (John 1:7)
17. The Lawgiver, Who is Able to Save (James 4:12)
18. He Is Ready to Judge the Quick and the Dead (2 Timothy 4:1)
19. The Living and True God (1 Thessalonians 1:9)
20. The Just One (Acts 7:52)
21. The Light and the Redeemer of the World (Doctrine & Covenants 93:9)
22. Peniel (Genesis 32:30)
23. The Lord of the Sabbath (Mark 2:28)
24. (He) Who Was Made Lower than the Angels for the Suffering of Death (Hebrews 2:9)
25. The Lord Both of the Dead and Living (Romans 14:9)
26. The Chief Cornerstone (Ephesians 2:20)
27. A New and Living Way (Hebrews 10:20)
28. Our Father, our Redeemer (Isaiah 63:16)
29. A Great God and a Great King (Psalms 95:3)
30. (He Who was) Consecrated for Evermore (Hebrews 7:28)

December

1 Jesus of Nazareth (Matthew 26:71)
2 The Propitiation for our Sins (1 John 2:2)
3 One God and Father of All (Ephesians 4:6)
4 Christ (1 John 5:1)
5 The Heir of all Things (Hebrews 1:2)
6 The Chief Shepherd (1 Peter 5:4)
7 The King of Saints (Revelation 15:3)
8 He That Liveth and was Dead (Revelation 1:18)
9 A Great Light (Matthew 4:16)
10 The Light of the World (John 8:12)
11 The Fountain of the Water of Life (Revelation 21:6)
12 The Lord is a God of Knowledge (1 Samuel 2:3)
13 The Lord God of our Fathers (Deuteronomy 26:7)
14 Christ, Who is our Life (Colossians 3:4)
15 God Who Quickeneth all Things (1 Timothy 6:13)
16 He is Faithful and Just (1 John 1:9)
17 God is Faithful (1 Corinthians 10:13)
18 The Head of the Body (Colossians 1:18)
19 Christ, the Son of the Living God (Matthew 16:16)
20 The Most High over all the Earth (Psalms 83:18)
21 God the Father (1 Peter 1:2)
22 A Personage Whose Brightness and Glory Defy all Description (Joseph Smith History 1:17)
23 The Son of Mary (Mark 6:3)
24 The Express Image of God's Person (Hebrews 1:3)
25 A Holy Child (Moroni 8:3)
26 The Seed of the Woman (Genesis 3:15)
27 God's Holy Child Jesus (Acts 4:27)
28 The King of the Jews (Matthew 2:2)
29 The Firstfruits of them that Slept (1 Corinthians 15:20)
30 The King that Cometh in the Name of the Lord (Luke 19:38)
31 Him Which is Perfect in Knowledge (Job 37:16)

Minute Musings

Spontaneous Combustions of Thought

Volume One

Appendix Two

An Alphabetical List of
366 Scriptural References to Jesus Christ

"That which cometh from above is sacred, and must be
spoken with care, and by constraint of the Spirit."
(Doctrine & Covenants 63:64).

compiled by

Philip M. Hudson

A
Abba, Father (Mark 14:36) (February 14)
Able to Save to the Uttermost (Hebrews 7:25) (January 11)
Able to Succor them that are Tempted (Hebrews 2:18) (March 1)
Advocate with the Father (1 John 2:1) (May 1)
Almighty (Revelation 1:8) (August 9)
Almighty God (Genesis 17:1) (August 21)
Alpha and Omega   (Revelation 1:11) (July 28)
Amen (John 14:6) (January 27)
Anointed One (Psalms 2:2) (April 15)
Apostle (Hebrews 3:1)) (April 24)
Apostle and High Priest of our Profession (Hebrews 3:1) (September 21)
Author (Moroni 6:4) (October 25)
Author and Finisher of our Faith (Hebrews 12:2) (April 16)
Author of Eternal Salvation (Hebrews 5:9) (August 27)

B
Bare our Sins in His Own Body (1 Peter 2:24) (November 13)
Beginning and the End (Revelation 22:13) (February 23)
Beloved and Chosen from the Beginning (Moses 4:2) (October 30)
Beloved Son of God (Matthew 3:17) (March 2)
Better than the Angels (Hebrews 1:4) (August 10)
Bishop of your Souls (2 Peter 2:25) (July 29)
Blessed for Evermore (2 Corinthians 11:31) (October 1)
Blessed of God (Psalms 45:2) (September 5)
Branch (Isaiah 11:1) (July 25)
Brazen Serpent (Helaman 8:14) (January 23)
Bread of Life (John 6:35) (January 18)
Bridegroom (Matthew 9:15) (March 20)
Bright and Morning Star (Revelation 22:16) (April 6)
Brightness of God's Glory (Hebrews 1:3) (February 5)
By Himself Purged our Sins (Hebrews 1:3) (June 28)

C
Came by Water and Blood (1 John 5:6) (May 15)
Came into the World to Save Sinners (1 Timothy 1:15) (March 18)
Captain (2 Chronicles 13:12) (September 2)
Captain of [Our] Salvation (Hebrews 2:10) (October 24)
Carpenter (Mark 6:3) (January 17)
Carpenter's Son (Matthew 13:55) (November 6)
Chief Cornerstone (Ephesians 2:20) (November 26)
Chief Shepherd (1 Peter 5:4) (December 6)
Chosen of God (John 23:35) (March 27)

Christ (1 John 5:1) (December 4)
Christ Jesus (Romans 3:24) (September 1)
Christ of God (John 9:20) (October 3)
Christ, the Chosen of God (Luke 23:35) (March 19)
Christ the Lamb (Doctrine & Covenants 76:85) (June 4)
Christ, the Son of the Living God (Matthew 16:16) (December 19)
Christ, Who is our Life (Colossians 3:4) (December 14)
Consecrated For Evermore (Hebrews 7:28) (November 30)
Consolation of Israel (Luke 2:25) (March 10)
Counsellor (Isaiah 9:6) (January 15)
Counselor (2 Nephi 18:6) (June 11)
Counted Worthy of More Glory than Moses (Hebrews 3:3) (February 21)
Creator (1 Peter 4:19) (May 2)
Creator of Heaven and Earth (Jacob 2:5) (September 29)
Creator of Israel (Isaiah 43:15) (April 4)
Creator of the Ends of the Earth (Isaiah 40:28) (February 4)
Crowned with Glory and Honour (Hebrews 2:9) (September 3)

D
Deliverer (Romans 11:16) (September 20)
Did no Sin (1 Peter 2:22) (May 9)
Died and Rose Again (1 Thessalonians 4:14) (April 9)
Door of the Sheep (John 10:7) (October 21)

E
Emmanuel (Matthew 1:23) (July 19)
End of the Law for Righteousness (Romans 10:4) (June 17)
Eternal Life (1 John 5:11) (June 13)
Everlasting God (Isaiah 40:28) (January 6)
Everlasting Light (Isaiah 60:19) (October 18)
Example (John 13:15) (February 27)
Example of the Son (2 Nephi 31:16) (June 10)
Excellent is Thy Name (Psalms 8:1) (January 28)
Express Image of God's Person (Hebrews 1:3) (December 24)

F
Faithful (1 Corinthians 10:13) (December 17)
Faithful and Just (1 John 1:9) (December 16)
Faithful and True (Revelation 19:11) (May 11)
Faithful Witness (Revelation 1:5) (May 28)
Father (Acts 1:4) (June 22)
Father and the Son (2 John 1:9) (November 15)
Father of Heaven and of Earth (2 Nephi 25:12) (March 28)

Father of Lights (James 1:17) (January 26)
Father of Spirits (Hebrews 12:9) (November 7)
Fear of God (Genesis 20:11) (January 4)
Fellowservant (Revelation 22:9) (May 29)
First and the Last (Isaiah 44:6) (January 31)
First Begotten (Hebrews 1:6) (February 19)
First Begotten of the Dead (Revelation 1:5) (October 22)
Firstborn (Romans 8:29) (May 4)
Firstfruits of Them that Slept (1 Corinthians 15:20) (December 29)
Foreordained Before the Foundation of the World (1 Peter 1:20) (July 2)
Forerunner (Hebrews 6:20) (August 13)
Foundation of the Church (1 Corinthians 3:11) (July 20)
Fountain of Living Waters (Jeremiah 2:13) (July 3)
Fountain of the Water of Life (Revelation 21:6) (December 11)

G
Gave Himself for our Sins (Galatians 1:4) (January 8)
Gave Himself for Us (Titus 2:14) (March 5)
Given us Understanding that We May Know Him that is True (1 John 5:20) (August 20)
Glory of the God of Israel (Ezekiel 9:3) (May 30)
God (Malachi 1:11) (May 20)
God and Father of our Lord Jesus Christ (1 Peter 1:3) (August 19)
God and His Father (Revelation 1:6) (May 31)
God and the Father (James 1:27) (June 1)
God is Love (1 John 4:8) (April 25)
God of Abraham, the God of Isaac, the God of Jacob (Exodus 3:6) (May 27)
God of Beth-el (Genesis 31:13) (February 28)
God of Israel (2 Nephi 25:14) (March 24)
God of Knowledge (1 Samuel 2:3) (December 12)
God of my Rock, my Shield, and the Horn of my Salvation, my High Tower, and my Refuge, my Savior (2 Samuel 22:3) (July 5)
God of my Salvation (Psalms 18:46) (February 2)
God of the Hebrews (Exodus 5:3) (August 25)
God of the Whole Earth (Isaiah 54:5) (June 2)
God of thy Father (Genesis 46:3) (May 26)
God our Father and the Lord Jesus Christ (Romans 1:7) (July 21)
God our Savior (Jude 1:25) (June 27)
God over all the Earth (1 Nephi 11:6) (September 26)
God the Father (Jude 1:1) (December 21)
God, the Greatest of All (Doctrine & Covenants 19:18) (February 15)
God the Judge of All (Hebrews 12:23) (March 11)
God's Anointed (Acts 4:27) (March 25)

God's Holy Child Jesus (Acts 4:27) (December 27)
Good (Psalms 34:8) (April 22)
Good Shepherd (John 10:14) (May 13)
Governor that Shall Rule Israel (Matthew 2:6) (July 27)
Great and True Shepherd (Helaman 15:13) (June 26)
Great Creator (Jacob 3:7) (August 22)
Great God (Titus 2:13) (April 14)
Great God and a Great King (Psalms 95:3) (November 29)
Great Jehovah (Doctrine & Covenants 128:9) (March 30)
Great King (Malachi 1:14) (January 19)
Great Light (Matthew 4:16) (December 9)
Great Shepherd of the Sheep (Hebrews 13:20) (May 14)

H
He Who Died and Rose Again (1 Thessalonians 4:14) (April 9)
Head of Every Man (1 Corinthians 11:3) (February 25)
Head of the Body (Colossians 1:18) (December 18)
Head of the Church (Ephesians 5:23) (May 12)
Head Stone of the Corner (Psalms 118:22) (October 15)
Healeth the People   (2 Chronicles 3:20) (February 12)
Heavenly King (Mosiah 2:19) (September 8)
Heir of all Things (Hebrews 1:2) (December 5)
High and Lofty One that Inhabits Eternity (Isaiah 57:15) (April 2)
High Calling of God (Philippians 3:14) (September 11)
High Priest after the Order of Melchizedek (Hebrews 5:10) (May 16)
High Priest of Good Things to Come (Hebrews 9:11) (October 2)
Highest of All (Doctrine & Covenants 76:70) (October 6)
Holiest of All (Hebrews 9:3) (September 28)
Holy Child (Moroni 8:3) (December 25)
Holy, Holy, Holy (Isaiah 6:3) (February 9)
Holy One and the Just (Acts 3:14) (October 20)
Holy One of Israel (Psalms 89:18) (June 20)
Holy One, the Creator of Israel (Isaiah 43:15) (August 18)
Hope of His People (Joel 3:16) (October 8)
Hope of Israel (Acts 28:20) (February 22)

I
I Am (John 8:58) (September 12)
I Am That I Am (Exodus 3:14) (November 3)
I Am the Law, and the Light (3 Nephi 15:9) (May 17)
Image of God (2 Corinthians 4:4) (April 18)

J

Jehovah (Exodus 6:3) (October 17)
Jehovah, Mighty God of Jacob (Doctrine & Covenants 109:68) (October 4)
Jehovah, the Eternal Judge (Moroni 10:34) (April 7)
Jesus (Romans 3:26) (May 18)
Jesus Christ (Ephesians 2:20) (June 12)
Jesus Christ His Son (1 John 1:7) (May 10)
Jesus Christ of Nazareth (Acts 4:10) (February 10)
Jesus Christ the Righteous (1 John 2:1) (April 10)
Jesus Christ the Son of God, the Father of Heaven and Earth,
    the Creator of All Things from the Beginning (Mosiah 3:8) (October 7)
Jesus of Galilee (1 Timothy 2:5) (April 19)
Jesus of Nazareth (Matthew 26:71) (December 1)
Jesus the Son of God (Hebrews 4:14) (March 21)
Joseph's Son (Luke 4:22) (October 27)
Judge of All the Earth (Genesis 18:25) (January 2)
Judge of Both the Quick and the Dead (Acts 10:42) (August 3)
The Judge of Quick and Dead (Acts 10:42) (April 20)
Just One (Acts 7:52) (November 20)

K

Key of David (Revelation 3:7) (January 5)
King (Isaiah 6:5) (March 26)
King Eternal (1 Timothy 1:17) (March 7)
King of all the Earth (Psalms 47:7) (July 30)
King of Heaven (2 Nephi 10:14) (November 8)
King of Kings (Revelation 17:14) (July 26)
King of Saints (Revelation 15:3) (December 7)
King of Sion (Matthew 21:5) (July 6)
King of the Jews (Matthew 2:2) (December 28)
King that Cometh in the Name of the Lord (Luke 19:38) (December 30)
King, Whose name is the Lord of Hosts (Jeremiah 46:18) (February 29)
Knew no Sin (2 Corinthians 5:21) (July 15)

L

Lamb (Revelation 5:5) (July 8)
Lamb Slain from Before the Foundation of the World (Revelation 13:8) (April 26)
Lamb that was Slain (Revelation 5:12) (June 21)
Lamb without Blemish and without Spot (1 Peter 1:19) (July 31)
Law, and the Life, and the Truth (Ether 4:12) (October 23)
Lawgiver (Isaiah 33:22) (September 7)
Lawgiver, Who is able to Save (James 4:12) (November 17)
Learned Obedience by the Things Which He Suffered (Hebrews 5:8) (March 3)

Light (John 1:7) (November 16)
Light, and the Life, and the Truth (Ether 4:12) (April 27)
Light and the Redeemer of the World (Doctrine & Covenants 93:9) (November 21)
Light of Israel (2 Nephi 20:17) (August 4)
Light of Life (John 8:12) (October 28)
Light of Men (John 1:4) (March 13)
Light of the World (John 8:12) (December 10)
Light to Lighten the Gentiles (Luke 2:32) (September 22)
Liveth and Was Dead (Revelation 1:18) (December 8)
Living and True God (1 Thessalonians 1:9) (November 19)
Living Bread Which Came Down from Heaven (John 6:51) (August 14)
Living Father (John 6:57) (May 5)
Living God (Joshua 3:12) (April 30)
Living God and an Everlasting King (Jeremiah 10:10) (August 1)
Living Stone (1 Peter 2:4) (February 17)
Living Water (John 4:10) (March 15)
Lord (Matthew 28:6) (October 13)
Lord and Saviour (2 Peter 3:2) (July 7)
Lord and Savior Jesus Christ (2 Peter 2:20) (December 13)
Lord both of the Dead and Living (Romans 14:9) (November 25)
Lord even of the Sabbath (Matthew 12:8) (July 24)
Lord, for He is our God (Joshua 24:18) (August 28)
Lord from Heaven (1 Corinthians 15:47) (January 12)
Lord God (Jude 1:4) (August 12)
Lord God Almighty (2 Nephi 28:15) (April 29)
Lord God of Abraham (Genesis 28:13) (July 10)
Lord God of Hosts (Isaiah 10:24) (February 24)
Lord God of the Hebrews (Exodus 7:16) (May 19)
Lord God of the Holy Prophets (Revelation 22:6) (February 6)
Lord God of your Fathers (Deuteronomy 1:11) (August 30)
Lord God Omnipotent (Mosiah 3:21) (June 15)
Lord He is God (Deuteronomy 4:35) (January 10)
Lord is my Helper (Hebrews 13:6) (November 10)
Lord is our Judge; the Lord is our Lawgiver (Isaiah 33:22) (February 7)
Lord is the Strength of my Life (Psalms 27:1) (July 16)
Lord Jehovah (Isaiah 12:2) (August 23)
Lord Jesus (Luke 24:3) (March 4)
Lord of All (Acts 10:36) (October 5)
Lord of Glory (James 2:1) (March 16)
Lord of Heaven and Earth (Matthew 11:25) (April 28)
Lord of Hosts (Isaiah 5:16) (September 19)
Lord of Lords (1 Timothy 6:15) (June 3)
Lord of the Sabbath (Mark 2:28) (November 23)

Lord of the Vineyard (Jacob 5:75) (June 24)
Lord of the Whole Earth (Doctrine & Covenants 55:1) (June 14)
Lord our God is One Lord (Deuteronomy 6:4) (January 22)
Lord our Righteousness (Jeremiah 23:6) (July 17)
Lord that Healeth (Exodus 15:26) (February 16)
Lord the God of Heaven (Jonah 1:9) (April 5)
Lord the King of Israel (Isaiah 44:6) (August 24)
Lord the Righteous Judge (2 Timothy 4:8) (January 20)
Lord your God (Deuteronomy 10:17) (May 3)
Lower Than the Angels For the Suffering of Death
   (Hebrews 2:9) (November 24)

M
Made Angels, Authorities, and Powers…Subject to Him (1 Peter 3:22) (August 17)
Made Higher than the Heavens (Hebrews 7:26) (July 18)
Master (Matthew 23:8) (November 4)
Mediator (1 Timothy 2:5) (June 29)
Mediator of a Better Covenant (Hebrews 8:6) (August 8)
Mediator of the New Covenant (Hebrews 12:24) (October 9)
Mediator of the New Testament (Hebrews 9:15) (August 31)
Merciful (2 Chronicles 30:9) (September 18)
Merciful and Faithful High Priest (Hebrews 2:17) (March 29)
Messenger of the Covenant (Malachi 3:1) (October 10)
Messiah (Daniel 9:25) (October 29)
Messias (John 4:25) (July 12)
Mighty God (Isaiah 9:6) (April 17)
Mighty God of Jacob (Psalms 132:2) (August 7)
Mighty One of Israel (1 Nephi 22:12) (November 9)
Mighty One of Jacob (Isaiah 60:16) (January 7)
Minister of the Circumcision for the Truth of God (Romans 15:8) (February 13)
Minister of the Sanctuary and of the True Tabernacle (Hebrews 8:2) (September 6)
Most High God (3 Nephi 11:17) (July 9)
Most High over all the Earth (Psalms 83:18) (December 20)
My Helper (Hebrews 13:6) (November 10)
My Rock and my Salvation (Psalms 62:2) (November 14)

N
Nazarene (Matthew 2:23) (January 30)
New and Living Way (Hebrews 10:20) (November 27)

O
Obtained Eternal Redemption for Us (Hebrews 9:12) (September 4)
Offered Himself Without Spot (Hebrews 9:11) (July 1)

Offering and Sacrifice to God (Ephesians 5:2) (September 16)
Omega (Revelation 1:11) (November 5)
One Eternal God (Alma 11:44) (October 11)
One God and Father of All (Ephesians 4:6) (December 3)
One Having Authority (Matthew 7:29) (July 4)
One With the Father (John 10:30) (September 13)
Only Begotten Son (John 1:14) (March 6)
Only Wise God our Savior (Jude 1:25) (March 9)
Our Father, our Redeemer (Isaiah 63:16) (November 28)
Our Passover (Hebrews 13:1) (August 6)

P
Passed into the Heavens (Hebrews 4:14) (February 11)
Peniel (Genesis 32:30) (November 22)
Perfect in Knowledge (Job 37:16) (December 31)
Personage Whose Brightness and Glory Defy all Description
    (Joseph Smith History 1:17) (December 22)
Prepared from the Foundation of the World (Ether 3:14) (January 14)
Prince of Life (Acts 3:15) (January 29)
Prince of Peace (Isaiah 9:6) (October 14)
Prince of the Kings of the Earth (Revelation 1:5) (September 9)
Prophet of Nazareth (Matthew 21:11) (January 13)
Prophet of the Highest (Luke 1:76) (June 19)
Propitiation for our Sins (1 John 2:2) (December 2)
Propitiation for the Sins of the Whole World (1 John 2:2) (September 24)
Propitiation through Faith (Romans 3:25) (November 11)
Put Away Sin by the Sacrifice of Himself (Hebrews 9:26) (May 22)

Q
Quickeneth all Things (1 Timothy 6:13)

R
Rabbi (John 1:38) (January 16)
Rabboni (John 20:16) (May 6)
Raised from the Dead (2 Timothy 2:8) (April 3)
Ready to Judge the Quick and the Dead (2 Timothy 4:1) (November 18)
Redeemer (Isaiah 59:20) (September 23)
Redeemer of Israel (John 11:25) (November 12)
Redeemer of the World (Doctrine & Covenants 93:9) (June 25)
Refiner's Fire (Malachi 3:2) (August 29)
Resurrection and the Life (John 11:25) (November 2)
Righteous Branch (Jeremiah 23:5) (April 23)

Righteous Judge (2 Timothy 4:8) (February 18)
Righteous Man (Luke 23:47) (January 3)
Rock (1 Samuel 2:2) (May 7)
Rock and their Salvation (1 Nephi 15:15) (September 14)
Rock of Heaven (Moses 7:53) (June 30)
Rock of His Salvation (Deuteronomy 32:15) (May 23)
Rock of my Strength (Isaiah 17:10) (September 30)
Root and the Offspring of David (Revelation 22:16) (February 8)
Root of David (Revelation 5:5) (June 23)

S
Salvation (2 Timothy 2:10) (July 22)
Savior (Matthew 1:21) (May 24)
Savior Jesus Christ (Mormon 3:14) (March 23)
Savior of the Body (Ephesians 5:23) (June 5)
Savior of the World (John 4:42) (April 11)
Seed of Abraham (Galatians 3:16) (July 11)
Seed of David (2 Timothy 2:8) (August 26)
Seed of the Woman (Genesis 3:15) (December 26)
Sent that we Might Live Through Him (1 John 4:9) (October 26)
Serpent of Brass (Alma 37:19) (April 21)
Shadow of Heavenly Things (Hebrews 8:5) (May 21)
Shepherd of Israel (Psalms 80:1) (May 25)
Shield (Genesis 15:1) (September 27)
Shiloh (Ezekiel 21:27) (October 12)
Sitteth on the Right Hand of God (Colossians 3:1) (April 1)
Son Jesus Christ our Lord (1 John 5:20) (June 9)
Son of David (Matthew 12:23) (March 12)
Son of God (Romans 1:4) (April 8)
Son of Man (Matthew 16:27) (November 1)
Son of Mary (Mark 6:3) (December 23)
Son of the Blessed (Mark 14:61) (September 25)
Son of the Eternal Father (1 Nephi 13:40) (May 8)
Son of the Highest (Luke 1:32) (August 5)
Son of the Living God (Matthew 16:16) (June 16)
Son of the Most High God (Mark 5:7) (October 31)
Spirit of Truth (John 14:17) (June 8)
Spiritual Rock (1 Corinthians 10:4) (June 7)
Star out of Jacob (Numbers 24:17) (February 1)
Stone (Jacob 4:15) (August 2)
Stone of Israel (Genesis 49:24) (July 13)
Strength of Israel (1 Samuel 15:29) (March 22)
Strength of the Children of Israel (Joel 3:16) (January 24)

Suffered without the Gate (Hebrews 13:12) (January 25)
Sun of Righteousness (Malachi 4:2) (February 3)
Surety of a Better Testament (Hebrews 7:22) (March 17)

T
Tasted Death for Every Man (Hebrews 2:9) (February 20)
Teacher Come from God (John 3:2) (August 16)
There is One God, and One Mediator Between God and Man, the Man Christ Jesus (1 Timothy 2:51) (August 11)
Treasures of Wisdom and Knowledge (Colossians 2:3) (September 10)
True Light, Which Lighteth Every Man (John 1:9) (March 14)
True Vine (John 15:1) (March 31)

U
Unchangeable Priesthood (Hebrews 7:24) (September 15)
Uphold(s) all Things by the Word of His Power (Hebrews 1:3) (February 26)

V
Very Eternal Father of Heaven and of Earth (Alma 11:39) (October 16)

W
Way, the Truth, and the Life (John 14:6) (July 14)
Which is, and Which Was, and Which is to Come (Revelation 1:8) (June 6)
Without Sin unto Salvation (Hebrews 9:28) (March 8)
Witness of God (1 John 5:9) (August 15)
Wonderful (Isaiah 9:6) (January 1)
Word (John 1:1) (January 21)
Word of God (Revelation 19:13) (April 13)
Word of Life (1 John 1:1) (January 9)

Z
Zeal of the Lord of Hosts (2 Kings 19:31) (April 12)

Minute Musings

Spontaneous Combustions of Thought

Volume One

Appendix Three

An Alphabetical List of
1,098 Scriptural References to Jesus Christ

"That which cometh from above is sacred, and must be
spoken with care, and by constraint of the Spirit."
(Doctrine & Covenants 63:64).

compiled by

Philip M. Hudson

A

Abba, Father
(Mark 14:36) Volume 1 - February 14

Able to Deliver Us
(1 Nephi 4:3) Volume 2 – June 20

Able to Save to the Uttermost
(Hebrews 7:25) Volume 1 - January 11

Able to Succor Them That are Tempted
(Hebrews 2:18) Volume 1 - March 1

Above All
(1 Nephi 11:6) Volume 2 – June 21

Above all Things
(Doctrine & Covenants 88:41) Volume 3 – August 30

Advocate
(1 John 2:1) Volume 2 – August 15

Advocate with the Father
(1 John 2:1) Volume 1 - May 1

All-powerful Creator of Earth
(Jacob 2:5) Volume 3 – November 29

All-powerful Creator of Heaven
(Jacob 2:5) Volume 3 – November 28

All-powerful God
(Alma 44:5) Volume 3 – May 7

All Things came by Me
(Doctrine & Covenants 38:3) Volume 3 – November 12

All-wise Creator
(Mosiah 29:19) Volume 3 – March 17

Almighty
(Revelation 1:8) Volume 1 - August 9

Almighty God
(Genesis 17:1) Volume 1 - August 21

Almighty Power
(Mormon 9:26) Volume 2 – November 2

Alpha and Omega
(Revelation 1:11) Volume 1 - July 28

Alpha and Omega, even Jesus Christ
(Doctrine & Covenants 81:7) Volume 2 – December 22

Alpha and Omega, the Beginning and the End
(Doctrine & Covenants 61:1) Volume 3 – July 28

Alpha and Omega, your Lord and your God
(Doctrine & Covenants 75:1) Volume 2 – December 19

Alphus
(Doctrine & Covenants 95:17) Volume 2 – February 23

Amen
  (John 14:6) Volume 1 - January 27
Angel of the Lord
  (Zecharaiah 3:10) Volume 3 – May 19
Angry, O Lord
  (Alma 33:16) Volume 2 – October 1
Anointed One
  (Psalms 2:2) Volume 1 - April 15
Another Comforter
  (John 14:6) Volume 2 – June 10
Apostle
  (Hebrews 3:1-2) Volume 1 - April 24
Apostle and High Priest of our Profession
  (Hebrews 3:1) Volume 1 - September 21
Appears in the Presence of God for Us
  (Hebrews 9:24) Volume 2 – February 28
Arrow Shall go forth as the Lightning
  (Zechariah 9:14) Volume 2 – May 6
Author
  (Moroni 6:4) Volume 1 - October 25
Author and Finisher of our Faith
  (Hebrews 12:2) Volume 1 - April 16
Author of Eternal Salvation
  (Hebrews 5:9) Volume 1 - August 27

B
Bare our Sins in His Own Body
  (1 Peter 2:24) Volume 1 - November 13
Beginning and the End
  (Revelation 22:13) Volume 1 - February 23
Beginning of the Creation of God
  (Revelation 3:14) Volume 2 – March 21
Begotten of the Father
  (John 1:14) Volume 2 – March 28
Beloved and Chosen from the Beginning
  (Moses 4:2) Volume 1 - October 30
Beloved Son
  (2 Nephi 31:11) Volume 2 – March 29
Beloved Son of God
  (Matthew 3:17) Volume 1 - March 2
Beside Him there is no Savior
  (Doctrine & Covenants 76:1) Volume 3 – October 8

Better than the Angels
(Hebrews 1:4) Volume 1 - August 10
Bishop of your Souls
(2 Peter 2:25) Volume 1 - July 29
Blessed for Evermore
(2 Corinthians 11:31) Volume 1 - October 1
Blessed God
(Alma 19:29) Volume 2 – June 22
Blessed Jesus
(Alma 19:29) Volume 2 – June 23
Blessed of God
(Psalms 45:2) Volume 1 - September 5
Blood of Jesus Christ Cleanseth us from all Sin
(1 John 1:7) Volume 2 – April 11
Born of a Woman
(Alma 19:13) Volume 2 – June 24
Branch
(Isaiah 11:1) Volume 1 - July 25
Branch of the Lord
(2 Nephi 14:2) Volume 2 – June 25
Brazen Serpent
(Helaman 8:14) Volume 1 - January 23
Bread of God
(John 6:33) Volume 3 – May 31
Bread of Life
(John 6:35) Volume 1 - January 18
Bread Which came Down from Heaven
(John 6:41) Volume 3 – June 1
Bridegroom
(Matthew 9:15) Volume 1 - March 20
Bright and Morning Star
(Revelation 22:16) Volume 1 - April 6
Brightness of God's Glory
(Hebrews 1:3) Volume 1 - February 5
Builder
(Hebrews 11:10) Volume 3 – January 4
By Himself Purged our Sins
(Hebrews 1:3) Volume 1 - June 28
By Whom God Made the Worlds
(Hebrews 1:2) Volume 2 – April 12

C

Called us to Honor
(2 Peter 1:3) Volume 3 – November 26

Called us to Virtue
(2 Peter 1:3) Volume 3 – November 27

Called the Son of God, Because He Received not of the Fulness at the First
(Doctrine & Covenants 93:14) Volume 3 – June 19

Came by Water and Blood
(1 John 5:6) Volume 1 – May 15

Came down from Heaven
(John 6:51) Volume 3 – December 18

Came into the World to Save Sinners
(1 Timothy 1:15) Volume 1 – March 18

Cannot be Touched with the Feelings of our Infirmities
(Hebrews 4:15) Volume 3 – December 5

Captain
(2 Chronicles 13:12) Volume 1 – September 2

Captain of [their] Salvation
(Hebrews 2:10) Volume 1 – October 24

Carpenter
(Mark 6:3) Volume 1 – January 17

Carpenter's Son
(Matthew 13:55) Volume 1 – November 6

Causeth the Vapours to Ascend from the Ends of the Earth;
He Maketh Lightnings with Rain, and Bringeth forth the Wind
(Jeremiah 10:13) Volume 3 – June 15

Chief Cornerstone
(Ephesians 2:20) Volume 1 – November 26

Chief Shepherd
(1 Peter 5:4) Volume 1 – December 6

Child
(2 Nephi 19:6) Volume 2 – December 27

Chosen of God
(John 23:35) Volume 1 – March 27

Chosen of God and Precious
(1 Peter 2:4) Volume 2 – April 9

Christ
(1 John 5:1) Volume 1 – December 4

Christ a King
(Luke 23:2) Volume 3 – March 30

Christ – For so Shall He be Called
(Mosiah 15:21) Volume 2 – June 27

Christ for their Shepherd
  (Mormon 5:17) Volume 2 – October 27
Christ in God
  (Doctrine & Covenants 86:9) Volume 3 – June 20
Christ Jesus
  (Romans 3:24) Volume 1 – September 1
Christ of God
  (John 9:20) Volume 1 – October 3
Christ, the Chosen of God
  (Luke 23:35) Volume 1 – March 19
Christ, the Eternal God
  (2 Nephi 26:12) Volume 2 – January 7
Christ the King of Israel
  (Mark 15:32) Volume 3 – May 20
Christ the Lamb
  (Doctrine & Covenants 76:85) Volume 1 – June 4
Christ the Lord
  (Mosiah 16:15) Volume 2 – June 29
Christ, the Lord God Omnipotent
  (Mosiah 5:15) Volume 2 – June 28
Christ the Lord, Who is the Very Eternal Father
  (Mosiah 16:15) Volume 3 – August 17
Christ, the Power of God and the Wisdom of God
  (1 Corinthians 1:24) Volume 2 – January 20
Christ, the Savior of the World
  (John 4:42) Volume 3 – June 6
Christ the Son
  (Alma 11:44) Volume 2 – June 30
Christ, the Son of the Blessed
  (Mark 14:61) Volume 3 – January 12
Christ, the Son of the Living God
  (Matthew 16:16) Volume 1 – December 19
Christ, Who has Broken the Bands of Death
  (Mosiah 15:23) Volume 2 – July 1
Christ, Who is our Life
  (Colossians 3:4) Volume 1 – December 14
Christ, Who was before the World Began
  (3 Nephi 26:5) Volume 2 – October 26
Christ your Redeemer
  (Moroni 8:8) Volume 3 – December 1
Cometh in an Hour you Think Not
  (Doctrine & Covenants 51:20) Volume 3 – September 29
Cometh Quickly
  (Doctrine & Covenants 51:20) Volume 3 – September 28

Condescension of God
(1 Nephi 11:26) Volume 2 - July 2
Confidence of all the Ends of the Earth
(Psalms 65:5) Volume 2 - June 7
Consecrated for Evermore
(Hebrews 7:28) Volume 1 - November 30
Consolation of Israel
(Luke 2:25) Volume 1 - March 10
Controllest and Subjectest the Devil, and the Dark and Benighted Dominion of Sheol
(Doctrine & Covenants 121:4) Volume 3 - June 21
Counsellor
(Isaiah 9:6) Volume 1 - January 15
Counselor
(2 Nephi 18:6) Volume 1 - June 11
Counted Worthy of More Glory than Moses
(Hebrews 3:3) Volume 1 - February 21
Course is One Eternal Round
(Doctrine & Covenants 35:1) Volume 3 - October 15
Created the Heavens and the Earth
(Doctrine & Covenants 14:9) Volume 3 - September 25
Creator
(1 Peter 4:19) Volume 1 - May 2
Creator of all Things from the Beginning
(Mosiah 3:8) Volume 3 - March 20
Creator of Heaven and Earth
(Jacob 2:5) Volume 1 - September 29
Creator of Israel
(Isaiah 43:15) Volume 1 - April 4
Creator of the Ends of the Earth
(Isaiah 40:28) Volume 1 - February 4
Creator of the First Day, the Beginning and the End
(Doctrine & Covenants 95:7) Volume 3 - March 23
Crowned with Glory and Honour
(Hebrews 2:9) Volume 1 - September 3
Crucified for the Sins of the World
(Doctrine & Covenants 54:1) Volume 3 - September 22

D
Delight to Honor those who Serve me in Righteousness and in Truth unto the End
(Doctrine & Covenants 76:5) Volume 3 - October 27
Deliverer
(Romans 11:16) Volume 1 - September 20

Deliverer from Death
  (Doctrine & Covenants 138:33) Volume 3 – October 19
Delivereth us from the Wrath to Come
  (1 Thessalonians 1:10) Volume 2 - February 29
Did no Sin
  (1 Peter 2:22) Volume 1 - May 9
Died and Rose Again
  (1 Thessalonians 4:14) Volume 1 - April 9
Door
  (John 10:9) Volume 3 – July 18
Door of the Sheep
  (John 10:7) Volume 1 - October 21

E
El
  (Bible Dictionary, p. 661) Volume 2 – June 12
El-elohe-Israel
  (Genesis 33:20) Volume 2 - April 18
Elohim
  (Bible Dictionary, p. 661) Volume 2 - May 22
Emmanuel
  (Matthew 1:23) Volume 1 - July 19
End of the Law for Righteousness
  (Romans 10:4) Volume 1 - June 17
Endless and Eternal is My Name
  (Moses 7:35) Volume 2 - April 8
Endless is My Name
  (Moses 1:3) Volume 3 – July 13
Established the World by His Wisdom
  (Jeremiah 10:12) Volume 3 – December 8
Eternal Father
  (Doctrine & Covenants 20:77) Volume 2 - February 13
Eternal Father of Heaven
  (Mormon 6:22) Volume 2 - October 29
Eternal Father of Heaven and Earth
  (Mosiah 15:4) Volume 2 - February 8
Eternal God
  (Doctrine & Covenants 121:32) Volume 2 - February 2
Eternal God, and the Messiah who is the Lamb of God
  (1 Nephi 12:18) Volume 3 – May 26
Eternal Head
  (Helaman 13:38) Volume 3 – August 29

Eternal is My Name
   (Moses 7:35) Volume 3 – August 22
Eternal Judge of Both Quick and Dead
   (Moroni 10:34) Volume 2 – February 7
Eternal King
   (Doctrine & Covenants 128:23) Volume 2 – December 28
Eternal Life
   (1 John 5:11) Volume 1 - June 13
Eternal Redemption for Us
   (Hebrews 9:12) Volume 2 - April 16
Ever Liveth to Make Intercession
   (Hebrews 7:25) Volume 2 - March 3
Everlasting Father
   (Isaiah 9:6) Volume 2 - March 1
Everlasting God, the Lord, the Creator of the Ends of the Earth
   (Isaiah 40:28) Volume 1 - January 6
Everlasting King
   (Jeremiah 10:10) Volume 3 – July 23
Everlasting Light
   (Isaiah 60:19) Volume 1 - October 18
Ever Liveth to Make Intercession
   (Hebrews 7:25) Volume 2 - March 3
Example
   (John 13:15) Volume 1 - February 27
Example of the Son
   (2 Nephi 31:16) Volume 1 - June 10
Excellent is Thy Name
   (Psalms 8:1) Volume 1 - January 28
Express Image of God's Person
   (Hebrews 1:3) Volume 1 - December 24

F
Faithful
   (1 Corinthians 10:13) Volume 1 - December 17
Faithful and Just
   (1 John 1:9) Volume 1 - December 16
Faithful and True
   (Revelation 19:11) Volume 1 - May 11
Faithful Creator
   (1 Peter 4:19) Volume 3 – March 18
Faithful Witness
   (Revelation 1:5) Volume 1 - May 28

Faithfulness [is] the Girdle of His Reins
   (Isaiah 11:5) Volume 1 - December 15
Father
   (Acts 1:4) Volume 1 - June 22
Father and I are One
   (3 Nephi 28:10) Volume 2 – February 4
Father also Which is in Heaven
   (Mark 11:2) Volume 3 – July 12
Father and the Son
   (2 John 1:9) Volume 1 - November 15
Father, and the Son, and the Holy Ghost
   (3 Nephi 11:27) Volume 2 - February 3
Father, even the Spirit of Truth
   (John 15:26) Volume 3 – April 5
Father is in Me
   (3 Nephi 9:15) Volume 3 – September 15
Father, Lord of Heaven and Earth
   (Luke 10:21) Volume 3 – April 8
Father of All
   (Ephesians 4:6) Volume 3 – July 29
Father of all Things
   (Mosiah 7:27) Volume 2 - July 3
Father of Circumcision
   (Romans 4:12) Volume 3 - April 7
Father of Glory
   (Ephesians 1:17) Volume 3 – January 16
Father of Heaven and Earth
   (Mosiah 3:8) Volume 3 – July 19
Father of Heaven and of Earth
   (2 Nephi 25:12) Volume 1 - March 28
Father of Lights
   (James 1:17) Volume 1 - January 26
Father of Mercies
   (2 Corinthians 1:3) Volume 3 – March 27
Father of our Lord Jesus Christ
   (2 Corinthians 1:3) Volume 3 – April 12
Father of Spirits
   (Hebrews 12:9) Volume 1 - November 7
Father of the Heavens and of the Earth, and all Things that in them Are
   (Ether 4:7) Volume 2 – November 4
Father of us All
   (Romans 4:16) Volume 3 – May 10
Father, Son, and Holy Ghost are One God, Infinite and Eternal, without End
   (Doctrine & Covenants 20:28) Volume 3 – June 23

Father which is in Heaven
(Matthew 10:33) Volume 3 – March 2
Fear of God
(Genesis 20:11) Volume 1 - January 4
Fear of Isaac
(Genesis 31:42) Volume 2 – April 2
Fellowservant
(Revelation 22:9) Volume 1 - May 29
Figure for the Time then Present
(Hebrews 9:9) Volume 2 - January 14
Finisher of their Faith
(Moroni 6:4) Volume 2 – November 12
Fire
(2 Nephi 20:17) Volume 2 - July 4
First and the Last
(Isaiah 44:6) Volume 1 - January 31
First Begotten
(Hebrews 1:6) Volume 1 - February 19
First Begotten of the Dead
(Revelation 1:5) Volume 1 - October 22
Firstborn
(Romans 8:29) Volume 1 - May 4
Firstborn from the Dead
(Colossians 1:18) Volume 3 – August 23
Firstborn Son
(Matthew 1:25) Volume 3 – December 20
First Fruits
(Doctrine & Covenants 88:98) Volume 3 – June 24
Firstfruits of them that Slept
(1 Corinthians 15:20) Volume 1 - December 29
Firstfruits unto God
(2 Nephi 2:9) Volume 3 – January 1
Flame
(2 Nephi 20:17) Volume 2 - July 5
Foreordained Before the Foundation of the World
(1 Peter 1:20) Volume 1 - July 2
Forerunner
(Hebrews 6:20) Volume 1 - August 13
Formed thee from the Womb
(Isaiah 44:24) Volume 3 – December 24
Foundation of the Church
(1 Corinthians 3:11) Volume 1 - July 20
Founder of Peace
(Mosiah 15:18) Volume 2 - November 21

Fountain of Living Waters
    (Jeremiah 2:13) Volume 1 - July 3
Fountain of the Water of Life
    (Revelation 21:6) Volume 1 - December 11
Framer of Heaven and Earth, and all Things which are in Them
    (Doctrine & Covenants 20:17) Volume 2 - December 20
From all Eternity to all Eternity
    (Moroni 8:18) Volume 3 – November 21
From Everlasting to Everlasting
    (Doctrine & Covenants 20:17) Volume 2 - November 30
Full of Equity
    (Alma 9:26) Volume 3 – December 26
Full of Grace
    (Alma 9:26) Volume 3 – October 31
Full of Grace and Truth
    (2 Nephi 2:6) Volume 2 - July 6
Full of Mercy
    (Alma 9:26) Volume 3 – November 4
Full of Patience
    (Alma 9:26) Volume 3 – November 3
Full of Truth
    (Alma 9:26) Volume 3 – November 2

G
Gave Himself for our Sins
    (Galatians 1:4) Volume 1 - January 8
Gave Himself for Us
    (Titus 2:14) Volume 1 - March 5
Gift of God
    (John 4:10) Volume 3 – June 5
Gift of His Son
    (Ether 12:11) Volume 2 - November 10
Given us Understanding that We May Know Him that is True
    (1 John 5:20) Volume 1 - August 20
Giveth Life to all Things
    (Doctrine & Covenants 88:13) Volume 3 – October 5
Giveth you Light
    (Doctrine & Covenants 88:11) Volume 3 – October 7
Glory and Virtue
    (2 Peter 1:3) Volume 2 - January 27
Glory of the God of Israel
    (Ezekiel 9:3) Volume 1 – May 30

Glory of the Lord
  (Ezekiel 1:28) Volume 3 – December 14
God
  (Malachi 1:11) Volume 1 - May 20
God an High Priest after the Order of Melchisedec
  (Hebrews 5:10) Volume 3 – January 10
God and Christ are the Judge of All
  (Doctrine & Covenants 76:68) Volume 3 – June 26
God and Father of our Lord Jesus Christ
  (1 Peter 1:3) Volume 1 - August 19
God and His Father
  (Revelation 1:6) Volume 1 - May 31
God and my Savior
  (3 Nephi 5:20) Volume 3 – October 24
God and our Father
  (Galatians 1:4) Volume 3 – April 24
God and Rock of their Salvation
  (Jacob 7:25) Volume 2 - July 7
God and the Father
  (James 1:27) Volume 1 - June 1
God and the Father of our Lord Jesus Christ
  (Colossians 1:3) Volume 2 - April 10
God and the Lamb
  (Doctrine & Covenants 76:119) Volume 3 – January 2
God, Even our Father
  (1 Thessalonians 3:13) Volume 3 – March 1
God, even the Father
  (James 3:9) Volume 3 – March 16
God in Heaven
  (Joseph Smith Matthew 1:40) Volume 3 – March 4
God in Heaven, Who is Infinite and Eternal
  (Doctrine & Covenants 20:17) Volume 3 – June 27
God in the Highest
  (Luke 2:14) Volume 2 - January 29
God is Judge Himself
  (Psalms 50:6) Volume 3 – March 25
God is Light
  (1 John 5:3) Volume 3- February 6
God is Love
  (1 John 4:8) Volume 1 - April 25
God is Merciful
  (Doctrine & Covenants 2:10) Volume 2 – December 1
God is Mindful of every People
  (Alma 26:37) Volume 2 - July 8

God is with Us
   (Alma 56:46) Volume 2 - July 9
God is with Thee in all that Thou Doest
   (Genesis 21:22) Volume 3 – November 20
God is with You
   (Zechariah 8:23) Volume 3 – December 6
God Manifest in the Flesh
   (1 Timothy 3:16) Volume 2 - March 2
God of Abraham, the God of Isaac, the God of Jacob
   (Exodus 3:6) Volume 1 - May 27
God of all Comfort
   (2 Corinthians 1:3) Volume 3 – March 28
God of Beth-el
   (Genesis 31:13) Volume 1 - February 28
God of Glory
   (Moses 1:20) Volume 2 - January 9
God of Gods
   (Deuteronomy 10:176) Volume 2 - January 28
God of Heaven
   (Moses 7:28) Volume 2 -   February 10
God of Israel
   (2 Nephi 25:14) Volume 1 - March 24
God of Israel Shall be your Rearward
   (3 Nephi 20:42) Volume 2 - October 21
God of Israel, Who is the Lord of Hosts
   (1 Nephi 20:2) Volume 2 - July 10
God of Jeshurun
   (Deuteronomy 33:26) Volume 3 – March 3
God of Knowledge
   (1 Samuel 2:3) Volume 1 - December 12
God of Miracles
   (2 Nephi 28:6) Volume 2 – July 11
God of my Rock, my Shield, and the Horn of my Salvation, my High Tower, and my Refuge, my Savior
   (2 Samuel 22:3) Volume 1 - July 5
God of my Salvation
   (Psalms 18:46) Volume 1 - February 2
God of Nature
   (1 Nephi 18:12) Volume 2 – July 12
God of our Fathers
   (1 Nephi 19:10) Volume 2 – July 13
God of our Lord Jesus Christ, the Father of Glory
   (Ephesians 1:17) Volume 3 – May 9

God of our Salvation
(Psalms 65:5) Volume 2 - November 3
God of the Hebrews
(Exodus 5:3) Volume 1 - August 25
God of the Whole Earth
(Isaiah 54:5) Volume 1 - June 2
God of this People Israel
(Acts 13:17) Volume 2 - February 11
God of thy Father
(Genesis 46:3) Volume 1 – May 26
God our Father
(1 Thessalonians 1:1) Volume 3 – April 2
God our Father and Jesus Christ our Lord
(2 Timothy 1:2) Volume 2 – April 27
God our Father and the Lord Jesus Christ
(Romans 1:7) Volume 1 - July 21
God our Savior
(Jude 1:25) Volume 1 - June 27
God over all the Earth
(1 Nephi 11:6) Volume 1 - September 26
God the Eternal Father
(Doctrine & Covenants 20:77) Volume 2 – January 5
God the Father
(Jude 1:1) Volume 1 - December 21
God the Father and Christ Jesus our Lord
(2 Timothy 1:2) Volume 3 – March 14
God the Father and His Only Begotten Son, Jesus Christ
(Doctrine & Covenants 138:14) Volume 3 – June 28
God the Father and the Lord Jesus Christ our Saviour
(Titus 1:4) Volume 2 – April 13
God, the Greatest of All
(Doctrine & Covenants 19:18) Volume 1 - February 15
God the Judge of All
(Hebrews 12:23) Volume 1 - March 11
God Who Brought the Children of Israel out of the Land of Egypt
(Mosiah 7:19) Volume 2 – September 29
God Who was the God of Abraham, and Isaac, and Jacob
(Mosiah 7:19) Volume 2 – September 29
God will Deliver Us
(Alma 58:37) Volume 2 - July 14
God with Us
(Matthew 1:23) Volume 3 – June 14
God's Anointed
(Acts 4:27) Volume 1 - March 25

God's Holy Child Jesus
   (Acts 4:27) Volume 1 - December 27
Good
   (Psalms 34:8) Volume 1 - April 22
Good Shepherd
   (John 10:14) Volume 1 - May 13
Good unto Them that Wait for Him
   (Lamentations 3:25) Volume 3 – November 11
Governor that Shall Rule Israel
   (Matthew 2:6) Volume 1 - July 27
Gracious
   (Doctrine & Covenants 76:5) Volume 3 – December 13
Gracious and Merciful, Slow to Anger, and of Great Kindness
   (Joel 2:13) Volume 3 – November 30
Granted Salvation unto His People
   (Mosiah 15:18) Volume 2 - February 15
Great and Eternal Head
   (Helaman 13:38) Volume 2 - October 8
Great and True Shepherd
   (Helaman 15:13) Volume 1 - June 26
Great Creator
   (Jacob 3:7) Volume 1 - August 22
Great God
   (Titus 2:13) Volume 1 - April 14
Great God and a Great King
   (Psalms 95:3) Volume 1 - November 29
Great...Head
   (Helaman 13:38) Volume 3 – August 28
Great High Priest, that is Passed into the Heavens
   (Hebrews 4:14) Volume 2 - December 30
Great I Am, Alpha and Omega, the Beginning and the End
   (Doctrine & Covenants 36:1) Volume 3 – October 18
Great I Am, even Jesus Christ
   (Doctrine & Covenants 39:1) Volume 3 – June 29
Great Jehovah
   (Doctrine & Covenants 128:9) Volume 1 - March 30
Great Jehovah, the Eternal Judge of Both Quick and Dead
   (Moroni 10:64) Volume 3 – January 15
Great King
   (Malachi 1:14) Volume 1 - January 19
Great Light
   (Matthew 4:16) Volume 1 - December 9
Great Mediator
   (2 Nephi 2:28) Volume 2 - July 15

Great Mediator of all Men
(2 Nephi 2:27) Volume 2 – January 13
Great Shepherd of the Sheep
(Hebrews 13:20) Volume 1 – May 14
[A] Great Spirit
(Alma 18:26) Volume 2 – July 16
[The] Great Spirit
(Alma 18:3) Volume 2 – July 17
[This] Great Spirit, Who is God
(Alma 18:28) Volume 2 – July 18
[That] Great Spirit, Who knows all Things
(Alma 18:18) Volume 2 – July 19
Great, the Mighty God, Lord of Hosts, is His Name
(Jeremiah 32:18) Volume 3 – October 26

H

Hand of the Lord
(Ruth 1:13) Volume 3 – December 17
Hath an Unchangeable Priesthood
(Hebrews 7:24) Volume 2 – April 14
Hath given us Understanding that we may Know Him that is True
(1 John 5:20) Volume 2 – April 15
He Hath made the Earth by His Power
(Jeremiah 51:15) Volume 3 – August 16
He is a Man like Ourselves
(Doctrine & Covenants 129:1) Volume 2 – December 12
He is Above all Things, and In all Things, and is Through all Things, and is Round About all Things
(Doctrine & Covenants 88:41) Volume 2 – April 17
He is an Holy God; He is a Jealous God
(Joshua 24:19) Volume 3 – February 26
He is Full of Mercy, Justice, Grace and Truth, and Peace
(Doctrine & Covenants 84:102) Volume 3 – June 25
He is Harmless
(Hebrews 7:26 Volume 3 – September 9
He is in the Moon
(Doctrine & Covenants 88:8) Volume 3 – August 31
He is in the Sun
(Doctrine & Covenants 88:7) Volume 3 – September 3
He is Pure
(Moroni 7:48) Volume 2 – November 16
He is the Light of the Moon
(Doctrine & Covenants 88:8) Volume 3 – September 1

He is the Light of the Sun
   (Doctrine & Covenants 88:7) Volume 3 – September 4
He is the Power thereof by which (the Moon) was Made
   (Doctrine & Covenants 88:8) Volume 3 - September 2
He is the Power thereof by which (the Sun) was Made
   (Doctrine & Covenants 88:7) Volume 3 – September 5
He is the Same, and His Years never Fail
   (Doctrine & Covenants 76:4) Volume 2 - December 14
He Shall be Called by the Name of Christ
   (Mosiah 5:9) Volume 2 - July 20
He Shall be Called the Lord our Righteousness
   (Jeremiah 23:6) Volume 3 – December 15
He Shall be Called the Son of God
   (Mosiah 15:2) Volume 2 - July 21
He that Ascended up on High
   (Doctrine & Covenants 88:6) Volume 3 – June 30
He that Cometh in the Name of the Lord
   (Matthew 21:9) Volume 2 - March 5
He That Formed Thee from the Womb
   (Isaiah 44:24)   Volume 3 – January 23
He that Giveth Salvation unto Kings
   (Psalms 144:10) Volume 2 - April 28
He that Hath Cut Rahab
   (2 Nephi 8:9) Volume 2 – July 22
He that Hath the Key of David
   (Revelation 3:7) Volume 2 – April 21
He that is Born King of the Jews
   (Matthew 2:2) Volume 3 – December   21
He that is Holy
   (Revelation 3:7) Volume 2 – March 6
He was called the Son of God, Because He Received not of the Fulness at the First
   (Doctrine & Covenants 93:14) Volume 3 – June 19
He was in the Beginning, Before the World Was
   (Doctrine & Covenants 93:7) Volume 2 – April 19
He Who came unto His Own
   (Doctrine & Covenants 88:48) Volume 2 – April 22
He Who Controllest and Subjectest the Devil, and the Dark and Benighted Dominion of Sheol
    (Doctrine & Covenants 121:4) Volume 3 – June 21
He Who hath dried the Sea
   (2 Nephi 8:10) Volume 3 – July 4
He Who was Crucified for the Sins of the World
   (Doctrine & Covenants 54:1) Volume 3 – June 22

Head of Every Man
(1 Corinthians 11:3) Volume 3 – September 6
Head of the Body
(Colossians 1:18) Volume 1 - December 18
Head of the Church
(Ephesians 5:23) Volume 1 - May 12
Head of the Corner
(1 Peter 2:7) Volume 2 – February 12
Head Stone of the Corner
(Psalms 118:22) Volume 1 - October 15
Healeth the People
(2 Chronicles 3:20) Volume 1 - February 12
Heavenly Father
(Matthew 15:13) Volume 3 – October 17
Heavenly King
(Mosiah 2:19) Volume 1 - September 8
Heir of all Things
(Hebrews 1:2) Volume 1 - December 5
High and Lofty One that Inhabits Eternity
(Isaiah 57:15) Volume 1 - April 2
High Calling of God
(Philippians 3:14) Volume 1 - September 11
The High God
(Micah 6:6) Volume 3 – August 13
High God their Redeemer
(Psalms 78:35) Volume 3 – January 31
High Priest
(Hebrews 4:15) Volume 3 – December 6
High Priest after the Order of Melchizedek
(Hebrews 5:10) Volume 1 - May 16
High Priest For Ever after the Order of Melchisedec
(Hebrews 6:20) Volume 3 – January 7
High Priest of Good Things to Come
(Hebrews 9:11) Volume 1 - October 2
High Priest Which Cannot be Touched with the Feelings of our Infirmities
(Hebrews 4:15) Volume 3 – January 13
High Priest Who is Set on the Right Hand of the Throne of the Majesty in the Heavens
(Hebrews 8:1) Volume 3 – January 14
Highest
(Luke 1:35) Volume 3 – January 9
Highest of All
(Doctrine & Covenants 76:70) Volume 1 - October 6
Him that Bringeth Good Tidings
(Mosiah 15:18) Volume 2 – July 23

Him that Hath called us to Glory and Virtue
  (2 Peter 1:3) Volume 2 – January 27
Him that is True
  (1 John 5:20) Volume 2 – April 23
Him Who has all Power
  (Doctrine & Covenants 61:1) Volume 3 – July 1
Him Who has Ordained you from on High
  (Doctrine & Covenants 77:2) Volume 2 – December 3
Him Who is from all Eternity to all Eternity
  (Doctrine & Covenants 39:1) Volume 3 – July 2
His Holy Child, Jesus
  (Moroni 8:3) Volume 2 – November 17
His Holy Will
  (Moroni 7:2) Volume 2 – November 13
His Son, Jesus Christ
  (Moroni 7:48) Volume 2 – November 15
His Word
  (2 Nephi 19:8) Volume 2 – July 24
His Years Never Fail
  (Doctrine & Covenants 76:4) Volume 3 – September 6
Hole of the Pit from Whence ye are Digged
  (2 Nephi 8:1) Volume 3 – April 16
Holiest of All
  (Hebrews 9:3) Volume 1 - September 28
Holiness of Jesus Christ
  (Mormon 9:5) Volume 2 – October 31
Holiness unto the Lord
  (Zechariah 14:20) Volume 3 – July 25
Holy
  (Hebrews 7:26) Volume 3 – September 8
Holy Child
  (Moroni 8:3) Volume 1 - December 25
Holy Child, Jesus
  (Moroni 8:3) Volume 2 – November 17
Holy Father
  (John 17:11) Volume 3 – April 30
Holy God
  (2 Nephi 9:39) Volume 2 – July 25
Holy, Harmess [and] Undefiled, Separate from Sinners, and Made Higher than the Heavens
  (Hebrews 7:26) Volume 2 – March 8
Holy, Holy God
  (Alma 31:15) Volume 2 – July 26

Holy, Holy, Holy
   (Isaiah 6:3) Volume 1 - February 9
Holy, Holy, Holy is the Lord of Hosts
   (2 Nephi 16:3) Volume 3 - February 19
Holy Messiah
   (2 Nephi 2:6) Volume 2 – April 4
Holy One
   (Isaiah 43:15) Volume 2 – March 7
Holy One and the Just
  (Acts 3:14) Volume 1 - October 20
Holy One of God
   (Mark 1:24) Volume 3 – February 7
Holy One of Israel
   (Isaiah 1:4) Volume 1 - June 20
Holy One of Israel, the True Messiah, their Redeemer and their God
   (2 Nephi 1:10) Volume 3 – February 16
Holy One, the Creator of Israel
   (Isaiah 43:15) Volume 1 - August 18
Hope of Glory
   (Colossians 1:27) Volume 2 – March 9
Hope of His People
   (Joel 3:16) Volume 1 - October 8
Hope of Israel
   (Acts 28:20) Volume 1 - February 22
Horn of David
   (Psalms 132:17) Volume 2 – June 9
Horn of my Salvation
   (2 Samuel 22:3) Volume 3 – July 15
Hosanna in the Highest
   (Mark 11:10) Volume 3 – January 11

I
I Am
   (John 8:58) Volume 1 - September 12
I am a God of Miracles
   (2 Nephi 27:23) Volume 2 – July 27
I am also the Last
   (1 Nephi 20:12) Volume 3 – September 13
I am Come in My Father's Name
   (John 5:43) Volume 3 – March 9
I am God
   (Moses 7:35) Volume 2 – January 19

I am He
  (John 18:5) Volume 3 – September 11
I am He; I am the First, and I am also the Last
  (1 Nephi 20:12) Volume 2 - July 31
I am He of whom Moses Spake
  (3 Nephi 20:23) Volume 2 – October 20
I am He that Comforteth You
  (2 Nephi 8:12) Volume 2 - July 28
I am He that Gave the Law
  (3 Nephi 15:5) Volume 2 - October 16
I am He, the Beginning and the End, the Redeemer of the World
  (Doctrine & Covenants 19:1) Volume 3 – June 18
I am He who Covenanted with my People Israel
  (3 Nephi 15:5) Volume 2 – October 17
I am He who Liveth
  (Doctrine & Covenants 110:4) Volume 3 – July 3
I am He Who said — Other Sheep have I Which are not of this Fold
  (Doctrine & Covenants 10:59) Volume 2 - November 29
I am He Who spake in Righteousness
  (Doctrine & Covenants 133:47) Volume 2 – December 2
I am He Who Speaketh
  (Ether 4:8) Volume 2 - November 5
I am He Who was Slain
  (Doctrine & Covenants 110:4) Volume 2 - December 4
I am in the Father, and the Father in Me
  (3 Nephi 9:15) Volume 2 – October 11
I am Jesus Christ
  (Doctrine & Covenants 51:20) Volume 3 – September 27
I am Jesus Christ the Son of God
  (Doctrine & Covenants 35:2) Volume 3 – April 11
I am Jesus Christ, the Son of God, Who was Crucified for the Sins of the World
  (Doctrine & Covenants 35:2) Volume 2 – August 2
I am Jesus Christ the Son of the Living God
  (Doctrine & Covenants 14:9) Volume 3 – September 24
I am Jesus Christ, Who Cometh Quickly, in an Hour you Think Not
  (Doctrine & Covenants 51:20) Volume 2 - August 6
I am no Respecter of Pesons
  (Doctrine & Covenants 1:35) Volume 3 – July 11
I am not of this World
  (John 17:16) Volume 3 – June 10
I am One in the Father
  (Doctrine & Covenants 35:2) Volume 3 – May 16
I am That I am
  (Exodus 3:14) Volume 1 - November 3

I am the Almighty God
   (Genesis 17:1) Volume 3 – November 7
I am the Door
   (John 10:9) Volume 3 – June 2
I am the Father
   (Ether 4:12) Volume 2 – November 6
I am the Father and the Son
   (Ether 3:14) Volume 2 – April 26
I am the First
   (1 Nephi 20:12) Volume 3 – September 12
I am the Firstborn
   (Doctrine & Covenants 93:21) Volume 3 – September 21
I am the God of Israel
   (3 Nephi 11:14) Volume 3 – September 17
I am the God of the Whole Earth
   (3 Nephi 11:14) Volume 3 – September 18
I am the God of thy Fathers, the God of Abraham, the God of Isaac, and the God of Jacob
   (Acts 7:32) Volume 3 – May 3
I am the Law, and the Light
   (3 Nephi 15:9) Volume 1 - May 17
I am the Life and the Light of the World
   (Doctrine & Covenants 11:28) Volume 2 – December 6
I am the Light of the World
   (Doctrine & Covenants 11:28) Volume 3 – October 22
I am the Light which ye shall Hold Up
   (3 Nephi 18:24) Volume 2 – October 19
I am the Lord
   (Ezekiel 6:7) Volume 3 – September 19
I am the Lord, the God of all Flesh
   (Jeremiah 32:27) Volume 3 – August 15
I am the Lord thy God
   (2 Nephi 8:16) Volume 2 – April 24
I am the Lord thy God from the land of Egypt
   (Hosea 13:4) Volume 3 – May 14
I am the Lord your God dwelling in Zion, My Holy Mountain
   (Joel 3:17) Volume 2 – August 7
I am the Root and the Offspring of David
   (Revelation 22:16) Volume 3 – May 17
I am the Same that Came unto Mine Own, and Mine Own Received Me Not
   (Doctrine & Covenants 6:21) Volume 3 – January 6
I am the Same that Leadeth Men to all Good
   (Ether 4:12) Volume 2 – November 7

I am the Son
   (Ether 3:14) Volume 3 – September 16
I am the True Light that is in You
   (Doctrine & Covenants 88:50) Volume 2 – April 25
I am the True Light that Lighteth every Man that Cometh into the World
   (Doctrine & Covenants 93:2) Volume 2 – November 26
I am their Redeemer
   (Mosiah 26:26) Volume 3 – December 16
I am with the Faithful Always
   (Doctrine & Covenants 62:9) Volume 2 – November 27
I am your Sign
   (Ezekiel 12:11) Volume 3 – September 4
I, and the Holy Ghost are One
   (3 Nephi 11:36) Volume 2 – October 14
I bear record of the Father
   (3 Nephi 11:32) Volume 2 – October 13
I, God
   (Doctrine & Covenants 19:16) Volume 2 – January 18
I, Jesus Christ, your Lord and your God, and your Redeemer
   (Doctrine & Covenants 18:47) Volume 2 – August 9
I that Am the Lord thy God
   (Hosea 12:9) Volume 3 – November 15
I, the Lord
   (1 Nephi 20:15) Volume 2 – August 3
I, the Lord, am Merciful
   (Doctrine & Covenants 70:18) Volume 2 – December 5
I, the Lord, am Merciful and Gracious unto Those who Fear Me, and Delight to Honor those who Serve me in Righteousness and in Truth unto the End
   (Doctrine & Covenants 76:5) Volume 2 – August 27
I the Lord am thy God
   (Doctrine & Covenants 132:47) Volume 3 – May 11
I the Lord am thy Savior and thy Redeemer
   (2 Nephi 6:18) Volume 3 – September 20
I The Lord am thy Savior and thy Redeemer, the Mighty One of Jacob
   (Isaiah 60:16) Volume 3 – February 3
I the Lord God
   (Doctrine & Covenants 34:1) Volume 2 – January 23
I the Lord thy God am a Jealous God
   (Mosiah 13:13) Volume 2 – July 29
I was in the Beginning with the Father
   (Doctrine & Covenants 93:21) Volume 3 – November 5
I will be a God unto thee, and to thy seed after thee
   (Genesis 17:7) Volume 3 – December 19

I will be their God
   (Ezekiel 11:20) Volume 3 – November 14
I will be unto Ephraim as a Lion, and as a Young Lion to the House of Judah
   (Hosea 5:14) Volume 3 – July 24
Image of God
   (2 Corinthians 4:4) Volume 1 - April 18
Immanuel
   (Doctrine & Covenants 128:22) Volume 2 - March 10
In all Things
   (Doctrine & Covenants 88:41) Volume 2 – April 7
In the Beginning the Word was, for He was the Word, even the Messenger of Salvation
   (Doctrine & Covenants 93:8) Volume 2 – August 4
In whom is Salvation
   (2 Timothy 2:10) Volume 2 – April 29
Inhabits Eternity
   (Isaiah 57:15) Volume 3 – July 19
Is not the Lord in Zion?
   (Jeremiah 8:19) Volume 3 – December 29
Israel's God
   (Doctrine & Covenants 27:3) Volume 3 – July 30
It is I that hath Spoken it
   (Ether 4:19) Volume 2 – November 9

J
JAH
   (Psalms 68:3) Volume 2 – March 17
Jehovah
   (Exodus 6:3) Volume 1 - October 17
Jehovah, Mighty God of Jacob
   (Doctrine & Covenants 109:68) Volume 1 - October 4
Jehovah, the Eternal Judge
   (Moroni 10:34) Volume 1 - April 7
Jesus
   (Romans 3:26) Volume 1 - May 18
Jesus Christ
   (Ephesians 2:20) Volume 1 - June 12
Jesus Christ, even the Father and the Son
   (Mormon 9:12) Volume 2 – October 30
Jesus Christ His Son
   (1 John 1:7) Volume 1 - May 10
Jesus Christ is the Name which is Given of the Father
   (Doctrine & Covenants 18:23) Volume 3 – July 5

Jesus Christ of Nazareth
   (Acts 4:10) Volume 1 - February 10
Jesus Christ our Lord
   (2 Timothy 1:2) Volume 3 – August 26
Jesus Christ the Righteous
   (1 John 2:1) Volume 1 - April 10)
Jesus Christ, the Son of David, the Son of Abraham
   (Matthew 1:1) Volume 3 – June 12
Jesus Christ, the Son of God
   (2 Nephi 25:19) Volume 2 – August 1
Jesus Christ, the Son of God, the Father of Heaven and Earth, the Creator of all Things from the Beginning
   (Mosiah 3:8) Volume 1 – October 7
Jesus Christ, your Lord and your God
   (Doctrine & Covenants 18:47) Volume 3 – January 22
Jesus Christ, your Lord and your Redeemer
   (Doctrine & Covenants 15:1) Volume 3 – January 25
Jesus Christ, your Lord, your God, and your Redeemer
   (Doctrine & Covenants 27:1) Volume 3 – January 26
Jesus Christ, your Redeemer, the Great I Am
   (Doctrine & Covenants 29:1) Volume 3 – May 23
Jesus is the Christ
   (Moroni 7:44) Volume 2 – November 14
Jesus is the Very Christ
   (2 Nephi 26:12) Volume 2 – January 22
Jesus of Galilee
   (1 Timothy 2:5) Volume 1 - April 19
Jesus of Nazareth
   (Matthew 26:71) Volume 1 - December 1
Jesus of Nazareth the King of the Jews
   (John 19:19) Volume 3 – May 18
Jesus of Nazareth, the Son of Joseph
   (John 1:45) Volume 3 – June 8
Jesus our Lord
   (Romans 4:24) Volume 2 – March 11
Jesus, the King of the Jews
   (Matthew 27:37) Volume 3 – February 5
Jesus, the Mediator of the New Covenant
   (Doctrine & Covenants 107:19) Volume 2 – January 3
Jesus the Prophet of Nazareth of Galilee
   (Matthew 21:11) Volume 3 – December 23
Jesus the Son of God
   (Hebrews 4:14) Volume 1 - March 21

Jesus, thou Son of God
(Alma 36:18) Volume 2 – August 10
Jesus, thou Son of God Most High
(Luke 8:28) Volume 3 – January 17
Jesus Who is Called Christ
(Matthew 1:16) Volume 3 – June 13
Joseph's Son
(Luke 4:22) Volume 1 - October 27
Judge of All
(Hebrews 12:23) Volume 2 – March 12
Judge of All the Earth
(Genesis 18:25) Volume 1 - January 2
Judge of Both the Quick and the Dead
(Acts 10:42) Volume 1 - August 3
The Judge of Quick and Dead
(Acts 10:42) Volume 1 - April 20
Just God
(Alma 29:4) Volume 2 – August 11
Just Lord
(Zephaniah 3:5) Volume 2 – April 21
Just One
(Acts 7:52) Volume 1 - November 20

K
Key of David
(Revelation 3:7) Volume 1 - January 5
King
(Isaiah 6:5) Volume 1 - March 26
King Eternal
(1 Timothy 1:17) Volume 1 - March 7
King Immanuel
(Doctrine & Covenants 128:22) Volume 2 – April 26
King of all the Earth
(Psalms 47:7) Volume 1 - July 30
King of Glory
(Psalms 24:7) Volume 2 – February 27
King of Heaven
(2 Nephi 10:14) Volume 1 - November 8
King of Israel
(Matthew 27:42) Volume 2 – June 13
King of Kings
(Revelation 17:14) Volume 1 - July 26
King of Nations

(Jeremiah 10:7) Volume 3 – December 30
King of Righteousness
(Hebrews 7:2) Volume 3 – May 22
King of Saints
Revelation 15:3) Volume 1 - December 7
King of Sion
(Matthew 21:5) Volume 1 - July 6
King of the Jews
(Matthew 2:2) Volume 1 - December 28
King of Zion
(Moses 7:53) Volume 2 - April 6
King over All the Earth
(Zechariah 14:9) Volume 3 – July 6
King that Cometh in the Name of the Lord
(Luke 19:38) Volume 1 - December 30
Knew no Sin
(2 Corinthians 5:21) Volume 1 - July 15
Knoweth the Weakness of Man
(Doctrine & Covenants 62:1) Volume 3 – October 10

L
Lamb
(Revelation 5:5) Volume 1 - July 8
Lamb of God, Which Taken Away the Sin of the World
(John 1:29) Volume 3 – June 7
Lamb Slain from Before the Foundation of the World
(Revelation 13:8) Volume 1 - April 26
Lamb that was Slain
(Revelation 5:12) Volume 1 - June 21
Lamb without Blemish and without Spot
(1 Peter 1:19) Volume 1 - July 31
Law, and the Life, and the Truth
(Ether 4:12) Volume 1 - October 23
Lawgiver
(Isaiah 33:22) Volume 1 - September 7

Lawgiver, Who is Able to Save
(James 4:12) Volume 1 - November 17
Leadeth all Men to all Good
(Ether 4:12) Volume 1 – October 1
Learned Obedience by the Things Which He Suffered
(Hebrews 5:8) Volume 1 - March 3

Left us an Example
    (1 Peter 2:21) Volume 2 – April 30
Life
    (John 11:25) Volume 3 – August 6
Life of Men and the Light of Men
    (Doctrine & Covenants 93:9) Volume 2 – February 24
Life which is Endless
    (Mosiah 16:9) Volume 2 – August 12
Light
    (John 1:7) Volume 1 - November 16
Light and my Salvation
    (Psalms 27:1) Volume 2 – June 17
Light and the Life of the World
    (Doctrine & Covenants 39:2) Volume 2 – April 5
Light, and the Life, and the Truth of the World
    (Ether 4:12) Volume 1 - April 27
Light and the Redeemer of the World
    (Doctrine & Covenants 93:9) Volume 1 – November 21
Light in the Wilderness
    (1 Nephi 17:13) Volume 2 – August 13
Light into the World
    (John 12:46) Volume 3 – June 3
Light of Christ
    (Doctrine & Covenants 88:7) Volume 2 – May 1
Light of Israel
    (2 Nephi 20:17) Volume 1 - August 4
Light of Life
    (John 8:12)   Volume 1 - October 28
Light of Men
    (John 1:4) Volume 1 - March 13
Light of the Moon
    (Doctrine & Covenants 88:8) Volume 3 – September 1
Light of the Stars
    (Doctrine & Covenants 88:9) Volume 3 – October 2
Light of the World
    (John 8:12) Volume 1 - December 10
Light that is Endless
    (Mosiah 16:9) Volume 2 – June 11
Light to Lighten the Gentiles
    (Luke 2:32) Volume 1 - September 22
Light to the Gentiles
    (1 Nephi 21:6) Volume 2 – December 25
Light which Cannot be Hid in Darkness
    (Doctrine & Covenants 14:9) Volume 2 – December 7

Light which is in all Things, which Giveth Life to all Things
(Doctrine & Covenants 88:13) Volume 2 – May 21
Light which Shineth
(Doctrine & Covenants 88:11) Volume 3 – October 6
Light which Shineth in Darkness
(Doctrine & Covenants 6:21) Volume 2 – February 26
Light which Shineth in Darkness and the Darkness Comprehendeth it Not
(Doctrine & Covenants 39:2) Volume 2 – December 23
Light which Shineth, which Giveth you Light
(Doctrine & Covenants 88:11) Volume 2 – May 2
Lighteth every Man
(John 1:19) Volume 3 – August 12
Lighteth every Man that Cometh into the World
(Doctrine & Covenants 93:2) Volume 3 – September 23
Like Fuller's Soap
(Doctrine & Covenants 128:24) Volume 2 – December 8
Like unto Thee, O Lord, among the Gods
(Exodus 15:11) Volume 1 - April 12
Lion of the Tribe of Judah
(Revelation 5:5) Volume 2 – February 17
Liveth
(Doctrine & Covenants 110:4) Volume 2 – February 6
Liveth and was Dead
(Revelation 1:18) Volume 1 - December 8
Liveth For Ever and Ever
(Revelation 4:9) Volume 2 – March 20
Living and True God
(1 Thessalonians 1:9) Volume 1 - November 19
Living Bread
(John 6:51) Volume 3 – July 21
Living Bread which Came Down from Heaven
(John 6:51) Volume 1 - August 14
Living Father
(John 6:57) Volume 1 - May 5
Living God
(Joshua 3:10) Volume 1 - April 30
Living God and an Everlasting King
(Jeremiah 10:10) Volume 1 - August 1
Living Stone
(1 Peter 2:4) Volume 1 - February 17
Living Water
(John 4:10) Volume 1 - March 15
Long-suffering
(Alma 9:26) Volume 3 – November 6

Looked upon all the Sereaphic Hosts of Heaven, Before the World was Made
(Doctrine & Covenants 36:1) Volume 3 – October 21
Lord
(Matthew 28:6) Volume 1 - October 13
Lord and His Goodness
(Hosea 3:5) Volume 2 – October 6
Lord and Saviour
(2 Peter 3:2) Volume 1 - July 7
Lord and Savior Jesus Christ
(2 Peter 2:20) Volume 1 - December 13
Lord and your Redeemer
(Doctrine & Covenants 34:12) Volume 3 – October 30
Lord Both of the Dead and Living
(Romans 14:9) Volume 1 - November 25
Lord, even Alpha and Omega
(Doctrine & Covenants 54:1) Volume 3 – July 8
Lord Even of the Sabbath
(Matthew 12:8) Volume 1 - July 24
Lord, Even the Savior
(Doctrine & Covenants 133:25) Volume 2 – January 1
Lord, for He is our God
(Joshua 24:18) Volume 1 – August 28
Lord From Heaven
(1 Corinthians 15:47) Volume 1 - January 12
Lord God
(Jude 1:4) Volume 1 - August 12
Lord God Almighty
(2 Nephi 28:15) Volume 1 - April 29
Lord God Almighty, Maker of Heaven, Earth, and Seas, and of all Things that in Them are
(Doctrine & Covenants 121:4) Volume 3 – March 15
Lord God Almighty, the Most High God
(3 Nephi 4:32) Volume 3 – April 1
Lord God is my Strength
(Habakkuk 3:19) Volume 3 – October 4
Lord God of Abraham
(Genesis 28:13) Volume 1 – July 10
Lord God of Abraham, Isaac, and of Israel
(1 Chronicles 29:18) Volume 2 – May 3
Lord God of Gods
(Joshua 22:22) Volume 3 – October 30
Lord God of Hosts
(Isaiah 10:24) Volume 1 - February 24

Lord God of Israel
   (Luke 1:68) Volume 2 – June 19
Lord God of Israel our Father
   (1 Chronicles 29:10) Volume 2 – May 4
Lord God of Israel, under whose Wings thou art Come to Trust
   (Ruth 2:12) Volume 3 – July 22
Lord God of Israel was their Inheritance
   (Joshua 13:33) Volume 2 – October 13
Lord God of my Master Abraham
   (Genesis 24:12) Volume 3 – January 3
Lord God of the Inhabitants of Jerusalem, and of the Land of Israel
   (Ezekiel 12:19) Volume 3 – December 11
Lord God of our Fathers
   (Deuteronomy 26:7) Volume 1 - December 13
Lord God of the Hebrews
   (Exodus 7:16) Volume 1 - May 19
Lord God of the Holy Prophets
   (Revelation 22:6) Volume 1 - February 6
Lord God of your Fathers
   (Deuteronomy 1:11) Volume 1 - August 30
Lord God Omnipotent
   (Mosiah 3:21) Volume 1 - June 15
Lord God, the God of Abraham, the God of Isaac, and the God of Jacob
   (Alma 29:11) Volume 2 – August 18
Lord God, the Mighty One of Israel
   (Doctrine & Covenants 36:1) Volume 2 – December 9
Lord God Who is Almighty
   (Helaman 10:11) Volume 3 – May 24
Lord He is God
   (Deuteronomy 4:35) Volume 1 - January 10
Lord, He is the God
   (1 Kings 18:39) Volume 3 – April 17
Lord in Shiloh
   (1 Samuel 1:24) Volume 3 – November 22
Lord is a Man of War
   (Exodus 15:3) Volume 3 – April 22
Lord is Above all Gods
   (Psalms 135:5) Volume 3 – August 11
Lord is Among Us
   (Joshua 22:31) Volume 2 – April 20
Lord is Clean
   (Psalms 19:9) Volume 3 – April 26
Lord is God
   (Doctrine & Covenants 1:39) Volume 3 – March 7

Lord is God, and Beside Him there is no Savior
(Doctrine & Covenants 76:1) Volume 2 – December 10
Lord is Good unto them that Wait for Him
(Lamentations 3:25) Volume 3 – September 30
Lord is Gracious
(1 Peter 2:3) Volume 3 – February 22
Lord is Great
(Psalms 135:5) Volume 3 – March 24
Lord is His Name
(Jeremiah 33:1) Volume 3 – May 1
Lord is in His Holy Temple
(Habakkuk 2:20) Volume 3 – April 13
Lord is my Helper
(Hebrews 13:6) Volume 1 - November 10
Lord is my Light
(Psalms 27:1) Volume 3 – October 24
Lord is my Salvation
(Psalms 27:1) Volume 3 – December 17
Lord is my Shepherd
(Psalms 23:1) Volume 3 – February 20
Lord (is) my Strength, and my Fortress, and my Refuge in the Day of Affliction
(Jeremiah 16:19) Volume 3 – April 19
Lord is Near
(2 Nephi 7:8) Volume 2 – August 19
Lord is our Judge; the Lord is our Lawgiver
(Isaiah 33:22) Volume 1 - February 7
Lord is Perfect
(Psalms 19:7) Volume 3 – April 27
Lord is Pure
(Psalms 19:8) Volume 3 – April 28
Lord is the Strength of my Life
(Palms 27:1) Volume 1 - July 16
Lord is the True God, He is the Living God, and an Everlasting King
(Jeremiah 10:10) Volume 3 – December 31
Lord is their Savior and their Redeemer, the Mighty One of Israel
(1 Nephi 22:12) Volume 3 – May 15
Lord is their Savior and their Redeemer, the Mighty One of Jacob
(1 Nephi 21:26) Volume 3 – February 24
Lord is thy Keeper
(Psalms 121:5) Volume 3 – March 19
Lord is with Thee
(1 Nephi 17:55) Volume 2 – August 20
Lord is with Us
(Jeremiah 8:8) Volume 3 – December 28

Lord Jehovah
  (Isaiah 12:2) Volume 1 - August 23
Lord Jesus
  (Luke 24:3) Volume 1 - March 4
Lord Jesus Christ our Saviour
  (Titus 1:4) Volume 3 – May 5
Lord Jesus Christ, the Son of the Father
  (2 John 1:3) Volume 2 – January 4
Lord Jesus Christ their Redeemer
  (3 Nephi 10:10) Volume 3 – May 27
Lord Liveth
  (Jeremiah 5:2) Volume 3 – December 27
Lord, Lord
  (Luke 6:47) Volume 3 – March 8
Lord Mighty in Battle
  (Psalms 24:8) Volume 3 – March 21
Lord my God, mine Holy One
  (Habakkuk 1:12) Volume 3 – April 6
Lord of All
  (Acts 10:36) Volume 1 - October 5
Lord of all the Earth
  (Joshua 3:13) Volume 3 – May 8
Lord of Glory
  (James 2:1) Volume 1 - March 16
Lord of Heaven and Earth
  (Matthew 11:25) Volume 1 - April 28
Lord of Hosts
  (Isaiah 5:16) Volume 1 - September 19
Lord of Hosts is His Name
  (Isaiah 47:4) Volume 3 – January 27
Lord of Hosts is My Name
  (2 Nephi 8:15) Volume 2 – August 21
Lord of Hosts, that Judgest Righteously
  (Jeremiah 11:20) Volume 3 – October 25
Lord of Hosts, that Planted Thee
  (Jeremiah 11:17) Volume 3 – August 27
Lord of Hosts, that Triest the Righteous
  (Jeremiah 20:12) Volume 3 – August 20
Lord of Hosts, the God of Israel
  (Jeremiah 7:3) Volume 3 – November 1
Lord of Lords
  (1 Timothy 6:15) Volume 1 - June 3
Lord of Peace
  (2 Thessalonians 3:16) Volume 3 – May 4

Lord of Sabaoth
    (Doctrine & Covenants 95:7) Volume 2 – June 14
Lord of the Sabbath
    (Mark 2:28) Volume 1 - November 23
Lord of the Sacrifice
    (Leviticus 7:29) Volume 3 – April 4
Lord of the Vineyard
    (Jacob 5:75) Volume 1 - June 24
Lord of the Whole Earth
    (Doctrine & Covenants 55:1) Volume 1 - June 14
Lord Omnipotent
    (Mosiah 3:5) Volume 2 – June 15
Lord our God
    (Alma 58:41) Volume 3 – October 12
Lord our God is One Lord
    (Deuteronomy 6:4) Volume 1 - January 22
Lord our God, Who has Redeemed us and Made us Free
    (Alma 58:41) Volume 2 – August 23
Lord Our Righteousness
    (Jeremiah 23:6) Volume 1 - July 17
Lord Strong and Mighty
    (Psalms 24:8) Volume 3 – March 21
Lord that hath Mercy on Thee
    (3 Nephi 22:10) Volume 2 – October 23
Lord that Healeth
    (Exodus 15:26) Volume 1 - February 16
Lord that Maketh all Things
    (Isaiah 44:24) Volume 3 – January 24
Lord the God of Heaven
    (Jonah 1:9) Volume 1 - April 5
Lord the God of Hosts is His Name
    (Amos 4:13) Volume 3 – November 16
Lord the King of Israel
    (Isaiah 44:6) Volume 1 - August 24
Lord the Lord and thy God
    (Isaiah 51:22) Volume 3 – October 14
Lord, the Redeemer of all Men
    (Alma 28:8) Volume 2 – February 16
Lord, the Redeemer of Israel
    (Isaiah 49:7) Volume 3 – February 11
Lord, the Redeemer of Israel, His Holy One
    (Isaiah 21:7) Volume 3 – January 19
Lord the Righteous Judge
    (2 Timothy 4:8) Volume 1 - January 20

Lord, their God, their Redeemer
   (1 Nephi 17:30) Volume 3 – May 28
Lord their Redeemer
   (1 Nephi 19:18) Volume 3 – January 30
Lord thy God
   (Abraham 2:7) Volume 2 – January 26
Lord thy Redeemer, the Holy One of Israel
   (1 Nephi 20:17) Volume 3 – May 2
Lord Who Redeemed Abraham
   (2 Nephi 27:33) Volume 3 – April 25
Lord, Whose Name is the God of Hosts
   (Amos 5:27) Volume 3 – August 13
Lord will roar from Zion, and utter His Voice from Jerusalem
   (Amos 1:2) Volume 2 – August 8
Lord your God
   (Deuteronomy 10:17) Volume 1 - May 3
Lord your God, even Alpha and Omega, the Beginning and the End, Whose Course is One Eternal Round, the Same Today as Yesterday, and Forever, your God and your Redeemer
   (Doctrine & Covenants 35:1) Volume 2 – August 24
Lord your God, even Jesus Christ, the Great I Am, Alpha and Omega, the Beginning and the End, the Same which Looked upon the Wide Expanse of Eternity, and all the Seraphic Hosts of Heaven before the World was Made
   (Doctrine & Covenants 38:1) Volume 2 – August 25
Lord your God, even Jesus Christ, your Advocate, Who knoweth the Weakness of Man and how to Succor them who are Tempted
   (Doctrine & Covenants 62:1) Volume 2 – December 11
Lord's Christ
   (Luke 2:26) Volume 2 – June 17
Lower than the Angels For the Suffering of Death
   (Hebrews 2:9) Volume 1 - November 24

M
Made Angels, Authorities, and Powers…Subject to Him
   (1 Peter 3:22) Volume 1 – August 17
Made Higher than the Heavens
   (Hebrews 7:26) Volume 1 - July 18
Made Lower than the Angels for the Suffering of Death
   (Hebrews 2:7) Volume 1 – November 24
Made of a Woman
   (Galatians 4:4) Volume 2 – May 7
Made the Earth by His Power
   (Jeremiah 51:15) Volume 3 – February 29

Made under the Law
(Galatians 4:4) Volume 2 – May 8
Maker
(Hebrews 11:10) Volume 3 - March 31
Maker of Heaven, Earth, and Seas, and of all Things that in them Are
(Doctrine & Covenants 121:4) Volume 3 – July 9
Maker, thy Husband, the Lord of Hosts is His Name
(3 Nephi 22:5) Volume 2 – October 22
Majesty
(Hebrews 8:1) Volume 2 – February 19
Majesty on High
(Hebrews 1:3) Volume 2 – February 18
Man
(3 Nephi 11:8) Volume 3 – February 28
Man Approved of God
(Acts 1:22) Volume 3 – June 16
Man of Counsel is My Name
(Moses 7:35) Volume 2 – March 30
Man of Holiness
(Moses 7:35) Volume 2 – January 8
Marvelous Light of God
(Mosiah 27:29) Volume 2 – December 24
Master
(Matthew 23:8) Volume 1 - November 4
Master and Lord
(John 13:13) Volume 3 – June 4
Master in Heaven
(Colossians 4:1) Volume 3 – January 5
Master of the Vineyard
(Jacob 5:7) Volume 2 – February 20
Mediator
(1 Timothy 2:5) Volume 1 - June 29
Mediator between God and Men
(1 Timothy 2:5) Volume 2 – February 22
Mediator of a Better Covenant
(Hebrews 8:6) Volume 1 - August 8
Mediator of the New Covenant
(Hebrews 12:24) Volume 1 - October 9
Mediator of the New Testament
(Hebrews 9:15) Volume 1 - August 31
Meek and Lowly
(Matthew 21:5) Volume 2 – March 24
Merciful
(2 Chronicles 30:9) Volume 1 - September 18

Merciful and Gracious unto Those who Fear Me, and Delight to Honor those who Serve me in Righteousness and in Truth unto the End
   (Doctrine & Covenants 76:5) Volume 2 – August 27
Merciful and Faithful High Priest
   (Hebrews 2:17 Volume 1 - March 29
Merciful is our God
   (Alma 24:15) Volume 2 – August 26
Merciful, O God
   (Alma 33:4) Volume 2 – October 3
Messenger of Salvation
   (Doctrine & Covenants 93:8) Volume 2 – January 6
Messenger of the Covenant
   (Malachi 3:1) Volume 1 - October 10
Messiah
   (John 1:41) Volume 1 - October 29
Messiah, the King of Zion, the Rock of Heaven
   (Moses 7:53) Volume 2 – January 17
Messiah the Prince
   (Daniel 9:25) Volume 3 – May 25
Messiah Who is the Lamb of God
   (1 Nephi 12:18) Volume 3 – February 15
Messiah Who Should Come
   (1 Nephi 10:17) Volume 3 – February 18
Messias
   (John 4:25) Volume 1 - July 12
Mighty God
   (Isaiah 9:6) Volume 1 - April 17
Mighty God of Jacob
   (Psalms 132:2) Volume 1 - August 7
Mighty One of Israel
   (1 Nephi 22:12) Volume 1 - November 9
Mighty One of Jacob
   (Isaiah 60:16) Volume 1 - January 7
Mighty to Save
   (Doctrine & Covenants 133:47) Volume 3 – July 10
Mightier than all the Earth
   (1 Nephi 4:1) Volume 2 – August 28
Mightier than I
   (1 Nephi 10:8) Volume 2 – August 29
Minister of the Circumcision for the Truth of God
   (Romans 15:8) Volume 1 - February 13
Minister of the Sanctuary and of the True Tabernacle
   (Hebrews 8:2) Volume 1 – September 6

More Excellent Way
  (Ether 12:11) Volume 2 – November 11
Most High
  (Acts 7:48) Volume 3 – January 8
Most High God
  (3 Nephi 11:17) Volume 1 – July 9
Most High God, Possessor of Heaven and Earth
  (Genesis 14:19) Volume 2 – August 22
Most High over all the Earth
  (Psalms 83:18) Volume 1 – December 20
My Beloved Son, Which was my Beloved and Chosen from the Beginning
  (Moses 4:2) Volume 3 – March 12
My Deliverer and my Shield
  (Psalms 144:2) Volume 2 – August 17
My Fortress
  (Jeremiah 16:19) Volume 3 – October 28
My Fortress and my Deliverer
  (2 Samuel 2:22) Volume 2 – August 14
My God
  (2 Nephi 4:20) Volume 2 – August 30
My God and my Savior Jesus Christ
  (3 Nephi 5:20) Volume 3 – February 25
My God and your God
  (Moses 6:47) Volume 2 – January 30
My Great God
  (Alma 24:8) Volume 2 – September 1
My Heavenly Father
  (Matthew 15:13) Volume 3 – April 20
My High Tower
  (2 Samuel 22:3) Volume 3 – July 16
My Light and my Salvation
  (Psalms 68:3) Volume 2 – March 16
My Name's Sake
  (1 Nephi 20:9) Volume 2 – September 2
My Refuge in the Day of Affliction
  (Jeremiah 16:19) Volume 3 – October 29
My Refuge, my Savior
  (2 Samuel 22:3) Volume 3 – July 17
My Rock
  (3 Nephi 18:12) Volume 2 – October 18
My Rock and my Salvation
  (Psalms 62:2) Volume 1 – November 14
My Salvation
  (Psalms 27:1) Volume 3 – October 23

My Son
   (Psalms 2:7) Volume 2 – June 4
My Strength
   (1 Nephi 21:5) Volume 2 – September 3
My Strength, and my Fortress, and my Refuge in the Day of Affliction
   (Jeremiah 16:19) Volume 2 – May 9
My Well-beloved
   (2 Nephi 15:1) Volume 3 – March 11

N
Name is from Everlasting
   (Isaiah 63:16) Volume 2 – May 23
Name of Christ, or of God
   (Mosiah 25:23) Volume 2 – September 4
Name of the Lord
   (Genesis 4:26) Volume 2 – May 5
Nazarene
   (Matthew 2:23) Volume 1 - January 30
New and Living Way
   (Hebrews 10:20) Volume 1 - November 27

O
Obtained Eternal Redemption for Us
   (Hebrews 9:12) Volume 1 - September 4
Of Whom are all Things
   (1 Corinthians 8:6) Volume 2 – May 10
Offered Himself without Spot
   (Hebrews 9:11) Volume 1 – July 1
Offering and Sacrifice to God
   (Ephesians 5:2) Volume 1 - September 16
Offering to God
   (Ephesians 5:2) Volume 3 – July 26
Offspring of David
   (Revelation 22:16) Volume 3 – August 8
Omega
   (Revelation 1:11) Volume 1 - November 5
Omegus; even Jesus Christ your Lord
   (Doctrine & Covenants 95:17) Volume 2 – February 21
One
   (Doctrine & Covenants 50:43) Volume 2 – October 15
One Among you Whom ye know Not
   (1 Nephi 10:8) Volume 2 – September 5

One Body
   (1 Corinthians 12:12) Volume 2 – May 11
One Eternal God
   (Alma 11:44) Volume 1 - October 11
One Eternal Round, the Same Today as Yesterday and Forever, your God and your Redeemer
   (Doctrine & Covenants 35:1) Volume 2 - August 31
One Father, even God
   (John 8:41) Volume 3 – April 3
[There is but] One God
   (Alma 11:35) Volume 2 - September 6
[There is] One God
   (1 Timothy 2:5) Volume 3 – August 9
[They are] One God
   (Mosiah 15:4) Volume 2 - September 7
One God and Father of All
   (Ephesians 4:6) Volume 1 - December 3
One God, and One Mediator between God and Man, the Man Christ Jesus
   (1 Timothy 2:51) Volume 1 - August 11
One God and One Shepherd over All
   (1 Nephi 13:41) Volume 2 – March 18
One Having Authority
   (Matthew 7:29) Volume 1 - July 4
One Jesus
   (Acts 17:7) Volume 3 – February 10
One Lord Jesus Christ
   (1 Corinthians 8:6) Volume 3 – April 29
One Mediator between God and Man
   (1 Timothy 2:51)   Volume 3 – August 10
One Messiah
   (2 Nephi 25:18) Volume 2 – September 8
One Shepherd
   (3 Nephi 15:17) Volume 3 – February 17
One with the Father
   (John 10:30) Volume 1 – September 13
Only Begotten
   (Moses 3:18) Volume 2 – January 21
Only Begotten, even Jesus Christ
   (Moses 7:50) Volume 2 – January 24
Only Begotten of the Father, Full of Grace and Truth, even the Spirit of Truth
   (Doctrine & Covenants 93:11) Volume 2 – August 5
Only Begotten of the Father, Full of Grace, Equity, and Truth, Full of Patience, Mercy, and Long-suffering
   (Alma 9:26) Volume 2 – September 9

Only Begotten Son
    (John 1:14) Volume 1 - March 6
Only Lord God
    (Jude 1:4) Volume 3 – April 10
Only Wise and True God, and Jesus Christ, Whom He hath Sent
    (Doctrine & Covenants 132:24) Volume 2 – November 22
Only Wise God our Savior
    (Jude 1:25) Volume 1 - March 9
Our Father, even God
    (John 8:41) Volume 3 - August 1
Our Father, our Redeemer
    (Isaiah 63:16) Volume 1 - November 28
Our Father which art in Heaven
    (Matthew 6:9) Volume 3 – April 21
Our Great and Eternal Head
    (Helaman 13:38) Volume 3 – August 28
Our Great God
    (Alma 24:7) Volume 2 – September 10
Our Life
    (Colossians 3:4) Volume 2 – May 12
Our Lord and Savior Jesus Christ
    (Mormon 3:14) Volume 3 – February 23
Our Lord is above all Gods
    (Psalms 135:5) Volume 3 – March 29
Our Lord Jesus Christ, Who Sitteth on the Right Hand of His Power
    (Moroni 9:26) Volume 2 – November 19
Our Passover
    (Hebrews 13:1) Volume 1 - August 6
Our Peace
    (Ephesians 2:14) Volume 2 – March 26

P
Passed into the Heavens
    (Hebrews 4:14) Volume 1 - February 11
Peace of God
    (Alma 7:27) Volume 2 – September 11
Peniel
    (Genesis 32:30) Volume 1 - November 22
Perfect
    (3 Nephi 12:48) Volume 2 – December 26
Perfect in Knowledge
    (Job 37:16) Volume 1 - December 31

Perfected For ever they that are Sanctified
   (Hebrews 10:14) Volume 2 – February 5
Personage
   (Joseph Smith History 1:19) Volume 3 – February 27
Personage Whose Brightness and Glory Defy all Description
   (Joseph Smith History 1:17) Volume 1 – December 22
Potentate
   (1 Timothy 6:15) Volume 3- March 10
Potter
   (Isaiah 64:8) Volume 2 – May 13
Power and Spirit of God, which was in Jesus Christ
   (3 Nephi 7:21) Volume 2 – October 10
Power Thereof by which (the) Moon was Made
   (Doctrine & Covenants 88:8) Volume 3 – September 2
Power Thereof by which (the stars) were Made
   (Doctrine & Covenants 88:9) Volume 3 – October 3
Power thereof by which (the Sun) was Made
   (Doctrine & Covenants 88:7) Volume 3 – September 5
Precious
   (1 Peter 2:7) Volume 3 – August 18
Prepared from the Foundation of the World
   (Ether 3:14) Volume 1 - January 14
Prepared…To Redeem My People
   (Ether 3:14) Volume 2 – April 3
Priest Forever after the Order of Melchizedek
   (Psalms 110:4) Volume 2 – March 13
Prince and a Savior
   (Acts 5:31) Volume 2 – January 31
Prince of Life
   (Acts 3:15) Volume 1 - January 29
Prince of Peace
   (Isaiah 9:6) Volume 1 - October 14
Prince of the Kings of the Earth
   (Revelation 1:5) Volume 1 - September 9
[A] Prophet
   (Deuteronomy 18:15) Volume 2 – January 12
[The] Prophet
   (John 7:40) Volume 2 – May 14
Prophet of Nazareth
   (Matthew 21:11) Volume 1 - January 13
Prophet of the Highest
   (Luke 1:76) Volume 1 - June 19
Prophet that Should Come into the World
   (John 6:14) Volume 3 – May 30

Propitiation for our Sins
  (1 John 2:2) Volume 1 - December 2
Propitiation for the Sins of the Whole World
  (1 John 2:2) Volume 1 - September 24
Propitiation through Faith
  (Romans 3:25) Volume 1 - November 11
Purifier of Silver
  (Doctrine & Covenants 128:24) Volume 3 – November 10
Put Away Sin by the Sacrifice of Himself
  (Hebrews 9:26) Volume 1 - May 22

Q
Quickeneth all Things
  (1 Timothy 6:13) Volume 1 – December 15

R
Rabbi
  (John 1:38) Volume 1 - January 16
Rabbi, Thou art the Son of God, Thou art the King of Israel
  (John 1:49) Volume 3 – June 9
Rabboni
  (John 20:16) Volume 1 - May 6
Raised from the Dead
  (2 Timothy 2:8) Volume 1 - April 3
Raised up out of His Holy Habitation
  (Zechariah 2:13) Volume 3 – September 10
Ready to Judge the Quick and the Dead
  (2 Timothy 4:1) Volume 1 - November 18
Received the Fulness of the Father
  (Doctrine & Covenants 76:71) Volume 2 – November 23
Redeemed us and Made us Free
  (Alma 58:41) Volume 3 – October 13
Redeemer
  (Isaiah 59:20) Volume 1 - September 23
Redeemer and Deliverer from Death and the Chains of Hell
  (Doctrine & Covenants 138:23) Volume 3 – February 5
Redeemer and our God
  (Alma 61:14) Volume 3 - February 9
Redeemer, even Jesus Christ
  (Doctrine & Covenants 80:5) Volume 3 – April 9
Redeemer, even the Son Ahman
  (Doctrine & Covenants 78:20) Volume 3 – January 21

Redeemer is Strong; the Lord of Hosts is His Name
 (Jeremiah 50:34) Volume 3 – September 26
Redeemer of all Men
 (Alma 28:8) Volume 2 – September 12
Redeemer of Israel
 (John 11:25) Volume 1 – November 12
Redeemer of the World
 (Doctrine & Covenants 93:9) Volume 1 – June 25
Redeemer the Holy One of Israel
 (Isaiah 54:5) Volume 3 – February 2
Redeemer, the Mighty One of Israel
 (1 Nephi 22:12) Volume 3 – February 8
Redeemer, Who is Jesus Christ, the Son of God
 (3 Nephi 5:16) Volume 3 – February 13
Redeemer, your Lord, and your God
 (Doctrine & Covenants 10:70) Volume 3 – May 21
Redemption
 (1 Corinthians 1:30) Volume 3 – November 25
Refiner
 (Doctrine & Covenants 128:24) Volume 3 – November 9
Refiner and Purifier of Silver
 (Doctrine & Covenants 128:24) Volume 2 – December 13
Refiner's Fire
 (Malachi 3:2) Volume 1 – August 29
Resurrection and the Life
 (John 11:25) Volume 1 – November 2
Righteous
 (Moses 7:47) Volume 2 – January 25
Righteous art Thou, O Lord
 (Jeremiah 12:1) Volume 3 – October 9
Righteous Branch
 (Jeremiah 23:5) Volume 1 – April 23
Righteous Father
 (John 17:25) Volume 3 – April 15
Righteous Judge
 (2 Timothy 4:8) Volume 1 – February 18
Righteous Man
 (Luke 23:47) Volume 1 – January 3
Righteousness
 (1 Corinthians 1:30) Volume 3 – November 23
Roar from Zion, and utter His Voice from Jerusalem
 (Amos 1:2) Volume 3 – July 7
Rock
 (1 Samuel 2:2) Volume 1 – May 7

Rock and mine Everlasting God
   (2 Nephi 4:35) Volume 2 – September 13
Rock and their Salvation
   (1 Nephi 15:15) Volume 1 - September 14
Rock of their Salvation
   (Jacob 7:25) Volume 3 – August 24
Rock from whence ye are Hewn
   (2 Nephi 8:1) Volume 2 - September 14
Rock of Heaven
   (Moses 7:53) Volume 1 - June 30
Rock of his Salvation
   (Deuteronomy 32:15) Volume 1 - May 23
Rock of my Righteousness
   (2 Nephi 4:35) Volume 2 – September 15
Rock of my Strength
   (Isaiah 17:10) Volume 1 - September 30
Rock of Offense
   (1 Peter 2:8) Volume 2 – May 15
Rock of Offense to Both the Houses of Israel
   (Isaiah 8:14) Volume 2 – January 15
Rock of our Redeemer, who is Christ, the Son of God
   (Helaman 5:12) Volume 2 – March 22
Rock of their Salvation
   (Jacob 7:15) Volume 2 – February 25
Rock that is Higher than I
   (Psalms 62:1) Volume 2 – January 10
Root
   (Revelation 22:16) Volume 3 – August 7
Root and the Offspring of David
   (Revelation 22:16) Volume 1 - February 8
Root of David
   (Revelation 5:5) Volume 1 - June 23
Round about all Things
   (Doctrine & Covenants 88:41) Volume 2 – June 6
Ruler and a Deliverer
   (Acts 7:35) Volume 3 – July 12

S
Sacrifice for Sin
   (2 Nephi 2:7) Volume 2 – December 29
Sacrifice to God
   (Ephesians 5:2) Volume 3 – July 27

Safe Foundation
   (Jacob 4:15) Volume 3 – November 17
Salvation
   (2 Timothy 2:10) Volume 1 - July 22
Salvation of the Lord
   (1 Nephi 19:17) Volume 2 – September 16
Salvation unto the Ends of the Earth
   (1 Nephi 21:6) Volume 2 – September 17
Same, and His Years never Fail
   (Doctrine & Covenants 76:4) Volume 2 – December 31
Same Light that Quickeneth your Understanding
   (Doctrine & Covenants 88:11) Volume 2 – April 1
Same that Spake unto you from the Beginning
   (Doctrine & Covenants 8:12) Volume 2 – September 18
Same Today as Yesterday and Forever, your God and your Redeemer
   (Doctrine & Covenants 35:1) Volume 3 – October 16
Same Unchangeable God
   (Doctrine & Covenants 20:17) Volume 2 – November 24
Same which Came in the Meridian of Time unto Mine Own, and Mine Own Received Me Not
   (Doctrine & Covenants 39:3) Volume 2 – December 15
Same which have taken the Zion of Enoch into Mine Own Bosom
   (Doctrine & Covenants 38:4) Volume 2 – September 19
Same which Knoweth all Things, for all Things are Present before Mine Eyes
   (Doctrine & Covenants 38:2) Volume 2 – December 16
Same which Looked upon the Wide Expanse of Eternity
   (Doctrine & Covenants 36:1) Volume 3 – October 20
Same which Spake, and the World was Made, and all Things Came by Me
   (Doctrine & Covenants 38:3) Volume 2 – September 20
Same Yesterday, Today, and Forever
   (Hebrews 13:8) Volume 2 – March 27
Sanctification
   (1 Corinthians 1:30) Volume 3 - November 24
[Our] Savior
   (1 Timothy 2:3) Volume 2 – May 16
[The] Savior
   (Philippians 3:20) Volume 1 - May 24
Savior and thy Redeemer, the Mighty One of Jacob
   (Isaiah 60:16) Volume 3 – August 2
Savior Jesus Christ
   (Mormon 3:14) Volume 1 - March 23
Savior of Israel
   (Acts 13:23) Volume 2 – March 25

Savior of the Body
   (Ephesians 5:23) Volume 1 - June 5
Savior of the World
   (John 4:42) Volume 1 - April 11
Seed of Abraham
   (Galatians 3:16) Volume 1 - July 11
Seed of David
   (2 Timothy 2:8) Volume 1 - August 26
Seed of the Woman
   (Genesis 3:15) Volume 1 - December 26
Sent that we Might Live through Him
   (1 John 4:9) Volume 1 - October 26
Separate from Sinners
   (Hebrews 7:26) Volume 2 – May 17
Serpent of Brass
   (Alma 37:19) Volume 1 - April 21
Set on the Right Hand of the Throne of the Majesty in the Heaven
   (Hebrews 8:1) Volume 3 – December 7
Shadow of Heavenly Things
   (Hebrews 8:5) Volume 1 - May 21
Shadow of Things to Come
   (Colossians 2:17) Volume 2 – January 2
Shall Appear the Second Time without Sin unto Salvation
   (Hebrews 9:23) Volume 2 – May 19
Shepherd
   (Psalms 23:1) Volume 2 – March 19
Shepherd in the Land
   (Zechariah 11:16) Volume 2 – June 8
Shepherd of Israel
   (Psalms 80:1) Volume 1 - May 25
Shepherd of the Sheep
   (John 10:12) Volume 3 – February 21
Shield
   (Genesis 15:1) Volume 1 - September 27
Shiloh
   (Ezekiel 21:27) Volume 1 - October 12
Sitteth on the Right Hand of God
   (Colossians 3:1) Volume 1 - April 1
Sitteth on the Right Hand of His Power
   (Moroni 9:26) Volume 3 – November 8
Sitteth upon the Throne, even the Lamb
   (Doctrine & Covenants 88:115) Volume 2 – December 21
Son
   (Moses 5:15) Volume 2 – February 1

Son Ahman; or, in other words, Alphus
　　(Doctrine & Covenants 95:17)　Volume 3 – November 13
Son Jesus Christ our Lord
　　(1 John 5:20)　Volume 1 - June 9
Son of Abraham
　　(Matthew 1:1)　Volume 2 – June 18
Son of David
　　(Matthew 12:23)　Volume 1 - March 12
Son of God
　　(Romans 1:4)　Volume 1 - April 8
Son of Man
　　(Matthew 16:27)　Volume 1 - November 1
Son of Man is Lord also of the Sabbath
　　(Mark 2:28)　Volume 3 – February 1
Son of Mary
　　(Mark 6:3)　Volume 1 - December 23
Son of our Great God
　　(Alma 24:13)　Volume 2 – September 21
Son of Righteousness
　　(3 Nephi 25:2)　Volume 2 – October 25
Son of the Blessed
　　(Mark 14:61)　Volume 1 - September 25
Son of the Eternal Father
　　(1 Nephi 13:40)　Volume 1 - May 8
Son of the Everlasting God
　　(2 Nephi 11:32)　Volume 2 – September 22
Son of the Highest
　　(Luke 1:32)　Volume 1 - August 5
Son of the Living God
　　(Matthew 16:16)　Volume 1 - June 16
Son of the Most High God
　　(Mark 5:7)　Volume 1 - October 31
Son, the Only Begotten of the Father
　　(Alma 5:48)　Volume 2 – September 23
Spirit of Jesus Christ
　　(Doctrine & Covenants 84:45)　Volume 3 – March 5
Spirit of Truth
　　(John 14:17)　Volume 1 - June 8
Spiritual Rock
　　(1 Corinthians 10:4)　Volume 1 - June 7
Standard
　　(1 Nephi 21:22)　Volume 2 – September 25
Star Out of Jacob
　　(Numbers 24:17)　Volume 1 - February 1

Stem of Jesse
  (Isaiah 11:0) Volume 2 – January 11
Stone
  (Jacob 4:15) Volume 1 - August 2
Stone of Israel
  (Genesis 49:24) Volume 1 - July 13
Stone of Stumbling
  (1 Peter 2:8) Volume 2 – May 20
Stone upon which they might Build and have Safe Foundation
  (Jacob 4:15) Volume 2 – September 26
Strength of Israel
  (1 Samuel 15:29) Volume 1 - March 22
Strength of the Children of Israel
  (Joel 3:16) Volume 1 - January 24
Stretched out the Heavens by His Discretion
  (Jeremiah 10:12) Volume 3 – August 19
Stumbling Stone and Rock of Offense
  (Romans 9:33) Volume 2 – January 16
Suffered for Us
  (1 Peter 2:21) Volume 2 – March 23
Suffered Without the Gate
  (Hebrews 13:12) Volume 1 - January 25
Sun of Righteousness
  (Malachi 4:2) Volume 1 - February 3
Support
  (2 Nephi 4:20) Volume 2 – September 27
Supreme Being
  (Doctrine & Covenants 104:7) Volume 2 – February 9
Supreme Creator
  (Alma 30:44) Volume 3 – March 26
Surety of a Better Testament
  (Hebrews 7:22) Volume 1 - March 17
Swift Witness
  (3 Nephi 24:5) Volume 2 – October 24

T
Tabernacle of God
  (Doctrine & Covenants 93:35) Volume 3 – August 5
Tasted Death for Every Man
  (Hebrews 2:9) Volume 1 - February 20
Teacher Come from God
  (John 3:2) Volume 1 - August 16

Teaches the Way of God in Truth
    (Mark 12:14) Volume 3 - November 19
Tempted in all Points as we Are
    (Hebrews 4:15) Volume 2 – March 14
The Man Christ Jesus
    (1 Timothy 2:51) Volume 3 - July 31
There is but One God
    (Alma 11:35) Volume 2 – September 6
There is None other Name given under Heaven save it be this Jesus Christ
    (2 Nephi 25:20) Volume 2 – September 30
There is One God, and One Mediator between God and Men, the Man Christ Jesus
    (1 Timothy 2:5) Volume 1 - August 11
They are One God
    (Alma 22:18) Volume 2 – September 7
This is My Beloved Son, in Whom I am Well Pleased
    (Matthew 3:17) Volume 3 – March 13
Thou art God
    (Alma 22:18) Volume 2 – October 2
Thou art my God
    (Hosea 2:23) Volume 2 – September 24
Thou art the Son of God
    (John 1:49) Volume 3 – December 22
Thou, O Lord, art our Father, our Redeemer; Thy Name is from Everlasting
    (Isaiah 63:16) Volume 3 – January 20
Thou, Whose name alone is Jehovah, art the Most High over all the Earth
    (Psalms 83:18) Volume 2 - May 18
Thy Lord the Lord, and thy God
    (Isaiah 51:22) Volume 3 – May 6
Treasures of Wisdom and Knowledge
    (Colossians 2:3) Volume 1 - September 10
True
    (Matthew 22:6) Volume 3 – November 18
True and Faithful
    (2 Nephi 31:15) Volume 2 – October 4
True and Faithful Witness
    (Jeremiah 42:5) Volume 3 – December 10
True and Living God
    (1 Nephi 17:30) Volume 2 – October 5
True, and Teaches the Way of God in Truth
    (Matthew 22:6) Volume 2 – March 4
True Bread from Heaven
    (John 6:32) Volume 3 – March 6
True Light
    (1 John 2:8) Volume 3 – August 11

True Light that Lighteth every Man that Cometh into the World
   (Doctrine & Covenants 93:2) Volume 2 – November 26
True Light, which Lighteth every Man
   (John 1:9) Volume 1 - March 14
True Messiah
   (2 Nephi 25:18) Volume 3 – May 12
True Messiah, their Lord and their Redeemer
   (1 Nephi 10:14) Volume 3 – February 12
True Messiah, their Redeemer and their God
   (2 Nephi 1:10) Volume 3 - December 12
True Vine
   (John 15:1) Volume 2 – May 25
Truth
   (John 14:16) Volume 3 – August 14
Truth of God
   (2 Nephi 28:28) Volume 2 – August 16
Truth of the World
   (Ether 4:9) Volume 2 – November 8

U
Unchangeable Being
   (Mormon 9:19) Volume 2 – November 1
Unchangeable from all Eternity to all Eternity
   (Moroni 8:18) Volume 2 – November 18
Unchangeable Priesthood
   (Hebrews 7:24) Volume 1 - September 15
Undefiled
   (Hebrews 7:26) Volume 3 – December 9
Uphold(s) all Things by the Word of His Power
   (Hebrews 1:3) Volume 1 - February 26

V
Very Christ
   (2 Nephi 26:12) Volume 2 – February 14

Very Christ and the Very God
   (Mormon 3:21) Volume 2 – Octobeer 28
Very Eternal Father
   (Mosiah 16:15) Volume 3 – July 14
Very Eternal Father of Heaven and of Earth
   (Alma 11:39) Volume 1 - October 16
Very God of Israel
   (1 Nephi 19:7) Volume 2 – October 7

Vine
(John 15:1) Volume 1 - March 31
Voice
(3 Nephi 9:1) Volume 2 – November 20
Voice of Lightnings
(Doctrine & Covenants 88:90) Volume 2 – June 1
Voice of One Crying in the Wilderness
(Doctrine & Covenants 88:66) Volume 2 – May 26
Voice of Tempests
(Doctrine & Covenants 88:90) Volume 2 – June 2
Voice of the Day of the Lord
(Zephaniah 1:14) Volume 2 – December 14
Voice of the Lord
(3 Nephi 1:12) Volume 2 – October 9
Voice of the Waves of the Sea heaving Themselves Beyond their Bounds
(Doctrine & Covenants 88:90) Volume 2 – June 3
Voice of Thunderings
(Doctrine & Covenants 88:90) Volume 2 – May 31

W
Way, the Truth, and the Life
(John 14:6) Volume 1 - July 14
Which is, and Which Was, and Which is to Come
(Revelation 1:8) Volume 1 - June 6
Who is Passed into the Heavens
(Hebrews 4:14) Volume 2 – May 29
Who Knew no Sin
(2 Corinthians 5:21) Volume 2 – May 28
Who Shall Judge the Quick and the Dead
(2 Timothy 4:1) Volume 2 – May 27
Wisdom of God
(1 Corinthians 1:24) Volume 3 – August 4
Wisdom, Righteousness, Sanctification, and Redemption
(1 Corinthians 1:30) Volume 2 – March 15
With the Faithful Always
(Doctrine & Covenants 62:9) Volume 2 – November 27
With the Father from the Beginning
(3 Nephi 9:15) Volume 2 – October 12
Without Sin unto Salvation
(Hebrews 9:28) Volume 1 - March 8
Witness of God
(1 John 5:9) Volume 1 - August 15

Wonderful
   (Isaiah 9:6) Volume 1 - January 1
Word
    (John 1:1) Volume 1 - January 21
Word, even the Messenger of Salvation
   (Doctrine & Covenants 93:8) Volume 2 – December 17
Word of God
   (Revelation 19:13) Volume 1 - April 13
Word of Life
   (1 John 1:1) Volume 1 - January 9
Word of the Lord
   (Joshua 22:9) Volume 2 – March 31

Y
Young Child
   (Matthew 2:9) Volume 3 – June 17
Your Father also Which is in Heaven
   (Mark 11:2) Volume 3 – April 18
Your Father, and your God, and my God
   (Doctrine & Covenants 88:75) Volume 2 – May 30
Your Father which is in Heaven
   (Doctrine & Covenants 84:92) Volume 2 – November 28
Your Father, Who is in Heaven
   (Doctrine & Covenants 84:83) Volume 2 – December 18
Your God
   (Moroni 8:8) Volume 3 – December 3
Your Heavenly Father
   (Matthew 6:32) Volume 3 - April 23
Your King
   (John 19:14) Volume 3 – May 29
Your Lord
   (Moroni 8:8) Volume 3 – December 2
Your Lord and your God
   (Moroni 8:8) Volume 3 – February 14
Your Lord and your Redeemer
   (Doctrine & Covenants 34:12) Volume 3 – January 18
Your Redeemer, even Jesus Christ
   (Doctrine & Covenants 80:5) Volume 3 – January 28
Your Redeemer, your Lord, and your God
   (Doctrine & Covenants 10:70) Volume 3 – January 29

Z
Zeal of the Lord of Hosts
  (2 Kings 19:31) Volume 1 - April 12

Additional Name-Titles & Descriptions

Jesus Christ the Son of the Living God, the Savior of the World
 (Doctrine & Covenants 42:1

Jesus Christ, Who is the Son (Doctrine & Covenants 76:14)

Jesus Christ, Who shall Come (Alma 45:4)

Minute Musings

Spontaneous Combustions of Thought

Volume One

Appendix Four

A Numerical List of
Scriptural References to Jesus Christ
by Body of Scripture

"That which cometh from above is sacred, and must be
spoken with care, and by constraint of the Spirit."
(Doctrine & Covenants 63:64).

compiled by

Philip M. Hudson

References that are used in the three volumes
have been selected from the following bodies of scripture:

Old Testament
(221)

New Testament
(415)

Book of Mormon
(257)

Doctrine & Covenants
(181)

Pearl of Great Price
(22)

Bible Dictionary
(2)

Total Scriptural References
1,098

About the Author

Phil Hudson and Jan, his wife of 47 years, have 7 children and over 20 grandchildren. They enjoy whiling away summer days with their family at their cabin, on the shores of Priest Lake, the crown jewel of North Idaho. Phil had a successful family dental practice in Spokane, Washington for 43 years, before retiring in 2015. In his free time, if he and Jan are not visiting their loved ones, he can be found roaming through Pacific Northwest woods, boating on the lake, cycling up mountain passes, riding his motorcycle along forest trails, or snowbiking in winter's deep powder along the Selkirk Crest. He always seems to find the time to write down his thoughts on his laptop, but appreciates Isaac Asimov's frustration when he was asked: "If you knew that you only had 10 minutes left to live, what would you do?" Without hesitation, Asimov answered: "I'd type faster."

Also by the Author

Minute Musings: Volume Two
Minute Musings: Volume Three

Essays: Spray from The Ocean of Thought
Essays: Ripples on a Pond
Essays: Serendipitous Meanderings
Essays: Presents of Mind
Essays: Some Assembly Required

Non-hybrid Seeds of Thought

Book of Mormon Commentary: Born in The Wilderness
Book of Mormon Commentary: Voices From the Dust
Book of Mormon Commentary: Journey to Cumorah

Today, as I Think About my Savior
Daily Inspiration from Scriptural Symbols

Diode Laser Soft Tissue Surgery (Volume One)
Diode Laser Soft Tissue Surgery (Volume Two)
Diode Laser Soft Tissue Surgery (Volume Three)

These, and other titles, are available at online retailers.

www.ingramcontent.com/pod-product-compliance
Lightning Source LLC
Chambersburg PA
CBHW060505240426
43661CB00007B/921